The Ethics of Determining One's Own Death

The Ethics of Determining One's Own Death

Essays on Den Hartogh's *What Kind of Death*

Edited by
Gijs van Donselaar,
Peter Rijpkema, and
Henri Wijsbek

LONDON AND NEW YORK

This work was originally published by Amsterdam University Press as a special issue of *Filosofie en Praktijk* 45.1 (2024).

First published in 2025 by Amsterdam University Press Ltd.

Published 2025 by Routledge
4 Park Square, Milton Park, Abingdon, Oxon OX14 4RN
605 Third Avenue, New York, NY 10158

Routledge is an imprint of the Taylor & Francis Group, an informa business

© Authors / Taylor & Francis Group 2025

All rights reserved. No part of this book may be reprinted or reproduced or utilised in any form or by any electronic, mechanical, or other means, now known or hereafter invented, including photocopying and recording, or in any information storage or retrieval system, without permission in writing from the publishers.

Trademark notice: Product or corporate names may be trademarks or registered trademarks, and are used only for identification and explanation without intent to infringe.

ISBN: 9789048569250 (pbk)
ISBN: 9781003706052 (ebk)
NUR 737

Cover design: Coördesign, Leiden

DOI: 10.5117/9789048569250

Every effort has been made to obtain permission to use all copyrighted illustrations reproduced in this book. Nonetheless, whosoever believes to have rights to this material is advised to contact the publisher.

For Product Safety Concerns and Information please contact our EU representative: GPSR@taylorandfrancis.com
Taylor & Francis Verlag GmbH, Kaufingerstraße 24, 80331 München, Germany

Table of Contents

Short Preface 7
    Gijs van Donselaar, Peter Rijpkema, Henri Wijsbek

Self-Determination and Its Limits 9
    Wayne Sumner

Whose Life is it Anyway? Some Reflections on Den Hartogh's
What Kind of Death 21
    Thomas Mertens

Dual or Single Gauge? Govert den Hartogh's 'Dual-Track' Assisted
Death 31
    Isra Black

The Changing (and Multifaceted) Role of the Principle of Self-
Determination in the Dutch Euthanasia Practice 49
    Esther Pans

Like a Peat Fire. The Impact of the Right to Self-Determination on
the (Dutch) Law on Euthanasia 55
    Jurriaan de Haan

Work to Be Done: An Inquiry Concerning Legal Certainty in the
Fourth Evaluation of the Dutch Euthanasia Act 65
    Heleen Weyers

Fear, Incompetence and Death. Empirical Observations and
Ethical Concerns about Dying with Advanced Dementia 85
    Eva C. A. Asscher

Response to Comments 99
    Govert den Hartogh

This Kind of Death? The Practice of Self-Euthanasia Illustrated 119
    Ton Vink

Short Preface

Gijs van Donselaar, Peter Rijpkema, Henri Wijsbek[1]

In the beginning of 2024 a special issue of *Filosofie & Praktijk*, now also published in book-form by Amsterdam University Press, brought together the key contributions to the conference *The Ethics of End-of-life Decisions* that was held on September 22, 2023 at the University of Amsterdam. The conference was organized on the occasion of the publication of *What Kind of Death. The Ethics of Determining One's Own Death*, the new standard work on ethical and legal issues concerning end-of-life decisions, by professor Govert den Hartogh.

The book is the culmination of a long series of papers prof. Den Hartogh has written over the last 20 years on a wide range of subjects related to end-of-life decisions, including physician-assisted death, suicide, palliative care and sedation until death, which are examined from both an ethical and a legal perspective. The book is informed not only by prof. Den Hartogh's comprehensive knowledge of the literature in this field, as the more than fifty pages of cited literature attest to, but also by his practical work in the field. Among other things, he served for many years as a member of a Regional Review Committee for Euthanasia and Physician-Assisted Suicide, and as a member of the Health Council of the Netherlands, an independent scientific advisory body to the Dutch Parliament and ministers in the field of public health. He was also involved in several high-profile lawsuits on questions of physician-assisted death. Reflecting this broad expertise, prof. Den Hartogh's book sets a standard for the current state of the discussion and will be a benchmark for the discussion on this subject for years to come.

The conference *The Ethics of End-of-life Decisions* reflected the comprehensiveness of prof. Den Hartogh's approach, as the central themes of his book were discussed by a mixture of ethicists, legal and medical professionals. The following contributions were written in response to Den Hartogh's

---

1 We thank Ton Vink for his assistance.

Gijs van Donselaar, Peter Rijpkema, and Henri Wijsbek (eds), *The Ethics of Determining One's Own Death. Essays on Den Hartogh's What Kind of Death.*
Taylor & Francis Group, 2025
DOI: https://doi.org/10.5117/FEP2024.1.001.VINK

book and are published in this volume: Leonard Wayne Sumner: "Self-Determination and its Limits"; Thomas Mertens: "Whose life is it anyway? Some reflections on Den Hartogh's *What Kind of Death*"; Isra Black: "Dual or single gauge? Govert den Hartogh's 'dual-track' assisted death"; Esther Pans: "The changing (and multifaceted) role of the principle of self-determination in the Dutch euthanasia practice"; Jurriaan de Haan: "Like a peat fire. The impact of the right to self-determination on the (Dutch) law on euthanasia"; Heleen Weyers: "Work to Be Done: An Inquiry Concerning Legal Certainty in the Fourth Evaluation of the Dutch Euthanasia Act"; Eva Asscher: "Fear, incompetence and death. Empirical observations and ethical concerns about dying with advanced dementia"; Ton Vink: "This kind of death? The practice of self-euthanasia illustrated".

As prof. Den Hartogh notes in his concluding response, the various contributions provide a thorough examination of the major steps in the main argument for his so called 'dual track approach'. As such, this collection of essays provides a valuable auxiliary to the book and an important further step in the ongoing debate about patient self-determination and patient well-being as the basic values for an ethics of determining one's own death.

Self-Determination and Its Limits

Wayne Sumner

Abstract
Defences of assisted dying typically rely on two supporting values for the practice: patient self-determination (or autonomy) and patient benefit (or well-being). In this paper I explore the roles of these two values in Govert den Hartogh's *What Kind of Death. The Ethics of Determining One's Own Death*.

Keywords: self-determination, autonomy, benefit, well-being, suicide, euthanasia, assisted dying.

Introduction

Defences of assisted dying typically rely on two supporting values for the practice: patient self-determination (or autonomy) and patient benefit (or well-being). When both values are aligned — that is, when a decisionally capable person makes a fully informed and voluntary request, and where death will provide a means of escaping intolerable suffering — the case for the right to an assisted death becomes very strong. When one or the other is absent, whether because the person is not decisionally capable, or they have not made a fully informed and voluntary request, or the death promises no benefit, the case becomes much weaker (though it may still be possible to make it).

Treatments of these issues in the end-of-life literature tend to be distinguished by the way in which they deploy these two values and, in particular, the way in which they handle their interplay. What is distinctive about Govert den Hartogh's excellent new book is its self-conscious privileging of self-determination, as is evident from its subtitle. (Den Hartogh 2023) Early on in the book, the author accepts the suggestion by an anonymous

---

Gijs van Donselaar, Peter Rijpkema, and Henri Wijsbek (eds), *The Ethics of Determining One's Own Death. Essays on Den Hartogh's What Kind of Death.*
Taylor & Francis Group, 2025
DOI: https://doi.org/10.5117/FEP2024.1.003.SUMN

reviewer that his approach to these end-of-life issues is "Benelux-centred". (Den Hartogh 2023, p. xii) It is certainly characteristically Dutch. In the Netherlands, self-determination is built in to the very definition of euthanasia, which requires an explicit and voluntary request by the patient. Elsewhere in the world, the term is generally construed more broadly, to comprehend all cases in which death is intentionally brought about for the benefit of the patient. On that understanding, euthanasia partitions into two categories: voluntary and nonvoluntary. On the Dutch concept, nonvoluntary euthanasia is an oxymoron.

Besides this distinctive approach to the issues, Den Hartogh's book is noteworthy for the broad range of end-of-life topics that it covers, including: palliative care, continuous deep sedation, stopping eating and drinking, mental illness as a qualifying medical condition for euthanasia, death wishes of the very old, advance euthanasia directives, conscientious objection, and the appropriate design of a system of oversight and regulation.[1] However, the main line of the argument runs from ending one's life on one's own (suicide) to enlisting the assistance of others (euthanasia). My remarks will follow this argumentative line.

Suicide

Den Hartogh defends a right to suicide by locating it within the broader right of self-determination. This latter right, he says, protects "an area of private sovereignty" (p. 30) and "delineate[s] a private domain within which it is up to you to decide what you do." (p. 29) This rubric of privacy and sovereignty should remind us of another defence of individual liberty which famously declared that: "Over himself, over his own body and mind, the individual is sovereign." (Mill 2003, p. 94-95))

To this point, Den Hartogh and Mill are very much on the same page. However, they soon appear to part company. Den Hartogh says, of the right of self-determination, that it "means, in the first place, that other people have corresponding duties, at least the duty not to interfere in the execution of your plan. In the second place it means that the reasons why they shouldn't interfere are *content-independent* ones. They do not depend on the prudential or moral quality of your decisions." (2023, p. 29) In the

---

[1] The focus on self-determination, however, precludes consideration of cases in which this element is absent, including the intentional ending of the life of infants. These cases do not qualify as euthanasia within the Dutch legal definition of the term.

same vein, he says that the question whether you have a right to suicide "is largely independent of the prudential and even the moral evaluation of your decision: if you have the right to end your own life, you are free to do so, whatever others, wrongly or even rightly, think of it. You need no right to make a proper decision." (p. 28-9)

In *On Liberty* Mill considers two possible grounds for interfering with individual liberty: harm to self and harm to others. While he rejects the former, joining with Den Hartogh in opposing paternalism, he endorses the latter: only conduct "calculated to produce evil to some one else" can qualify for interference or regulation. (2003, p. 95)[2] By contrast, when Den Hartogh claims that the reasons why others should not trespass in your area of private sovereignty "do not depend on the prudential *or moral* quality of your decisions" (emphasis added) he presumably means that neither harm to self *nor harm to others* can be a legitimate reason for interference. If we assume that wronging others at least typically consists in harming them, then Den Hartogh's rejection of Mill's harm principle appears to entail that, as he sees it, the right of self-determination includes the right to do wrong.

If this result seems odd, it may be because it appears to contradict a familiar analysis of the nature of rights, derived from Wesley Hohfeld. (Hohfeld 1919) On this analysis, having the right to do something comprises, at the minimum, two essential normative elements: the liberty to do it (i.e. having no duty not to do it) and a claim against others to be left unimpeded in the doing of it.[3] Den Hartogh's conception of a right of self-determination seems to include only the claim and not the liberty.

Rather than pursuing this conceptual issue further on the abstract level, it will be more rewarding to see how it plays out for the specific case of suicide. Den Hartogh devotes an entire chapter to the phenomenon he labels "the invisibility of rational suicide". In the public consciousness, and also in the view of most suicidologists, suicides are always, or nearly always, the result of mental illness and characterized by three features: they are impulsive, spur-of-the-moment decisions, they are achieved by violent means (drowning, shooting, hanging, jumping from a high place, etc.), and the intent to kill oneself is concealed from others, including family and friends. Against the prevalence of this picture, Den Hartogh argues forcefully that suicide

---

2   It is important to note that, for Mill, harm to others is only a necessary condition for justified interference in liberty, not a sufficient one. Whether such interference is justified, all things considered, is to be determined by its overall balance of harms and benefits. By contrast, where only harm to self is involved, the question of justification never arises.

3   The right may contain other normative elements as well; for a full exposition of the Hohfeldian analysis of rights, see Sumner 1987.

need not have any of these features: it can be carried out by a person who is mentally stable, it can be well-considered and carefully planned, it can employ nonviolent means such as medication, and the plan to end one's life can be shared in advance with, and even assisted by, one's loved ones. In short: suicides can be rational. However, when they are rational in this way they are seldom reported as suicides, especially if the means adopted is the refusal of food and fluids.[4] Hence the invisibility of rational suicide.

So we have two kinds of suicide: those that are rational (well-considered, peaceful, shared with others) and those we may label irrational (my term, not Den Hartogh's) that are "quasi-impulsive, violent, and lonely". (2023, p. 51) The former need involve no harm to self, since they may facilitate escape from further suffering, in which case death may be a benefit. Neither need they involve any harm to others. At least in the ideal case, while the deceased will doubtless be mourned and missed, family and friends will have had an opportunity to prepare for their loss and may well regard the death as a release. By contrast, irrational suicides will frequently, perhaps typically, feature both kinds of harm. If the impulsivity of the act is the outcome of a bout of severe depression, then it will frequently not be based on a rational assessment of the prospects for improvement in one's life. Violent, and lonely suicides tend to skew young, which makes the loss of a potentially brighter future particularly tragic. As for harm to family and friends, the sudden and unexpected death of a loved one is likely to have a devastating emotional impact, leading to self-examination and recrimination. The loss of a potentially productive family member can also increase the burdens on survivors and leave the family in difficult financial straits.

Rational suicides fit readily in Mill's protected domain of liberty, but irrational suicides will usually violate the harm principle. Both types, however, appear to be accommodated by Den Hartogh's "area of private sovereignty". In particular, the fact that irrational suicides will typically be wrongful, by virtue of causing harm to others, does not appear to be sufficient to disqualify them. So they too will be protected by the individual's right of self-determination.

Something is clearly amiss here. How can Den Hartogh defend a person's right to inflict such harm on those around them? How can he think that there is an unrestricted right to suicide, including irrational suicide, that is derived from the right of self-determination? The answer in both cases, I think, is that he does not—not really. To see why, we need to be mindful of

---

4   Or if the chosen means is a request for euthanasia. In the Netherlands there are more than three times as many reported cases of euthanasia every year as registered suicides.

the context in which this step in his argument occurs. The second chapter of *What Kind of Death* is devoted to "determining the manner and time of your own death". The first four sections of the chapter deal with familiar topics in the end-of-life literature: what constitutes a "good death", the reasons people most frequently give for wanting to end their lives, and how death can be a benefit. Only with that background in place is the question raised whether there is a right to suicide, and only in the following chapter is the reality of irrational suicides acknowledged. In defending an apparently unrestricted right to suicide, it seems clear that Den Hartogh has in mind only suicides that are "non-violent, interactive and well-considered". (p. 327) It does indeed seem reasonable to say that the right to end your life in these cases "is largely independent of the prudential and even the moral evaluation of your decision". But that is because the question of harm to self or others does not arise.

If this analysis is correct, and Den Hartogh's right to suicide is implicitly limited to rational suicides, then it has powerful implications for his overall argument, according to which the right to end one's own life is based on self-determination alone, while the right to the assistance of others (including euthanasia) additionally requires that death be a benefit, for now it appears that benefit has already been implicitly presupposed in establishing the right to suicide. If so, then that right rests on both values, not just the one, and Den Hartogh's argument is less distinctively Dutch than it first appears.

Euthanasia

In the Netherlands, patients approved for euthanasia have the option of oral self-administration of the medication or intravenous administration by a physician. Nearly all choose the latter.[5] Since he (correctly) sees no ethical difference between the two practices, Den Hartogh elects to use the term "euthanasia" to cover both. (p. 89-90) I will follow him in this practice. His overall line of argument posits a significant ethical gap between the right to end your life yourself (which requires only self-determination) and the right to enlist the assistance of others (which additionally requires benefit). We have seen some reason to doubt whether the former right really does rest solely on self-determination, since the expectation of benefit seems to be implicitly assumed. But, setting that question aside for the moment,

---

5   In 2021, 2.5% of the total assisted deaths in the Netherlands were self-administered. *Annual Report 2021*, Regional Euthanasia Review Committees, 9.

we can ask why the right to be assisted with the act does not flow logically from the right to the act itself. Ordinarily, we would expect that entailment. If I have the right to search the market for a new house, then surely I also have the right to engage a real estate agent to assist me. No new ground for the latter right appears to be needed. So why is one needed for the right to euthanasia? If I have the right to end my own life, why do I not also have the right to ask a doctor for assistance?

Den Hartogh argues that the assumption of an entailment presupposes the principle *Volenti no fit injuria*: you cannot be wronged by an action to which you have consented. (p. 157) That is not to say that you cannot be *harmed* by such an action, only that your consent entails that no *wrong* has been done to you. The *Volenti* principle underlies the familiar doctrine of informed consent to medical treatment. Your inserting a probe into my colon would normally qualify as a serious invasion of my bodily integrity, but if I have consented to a colonoscopy then you do me no wrong by proceeding. Den Hartogh contends, however, that the principle does not apply to "the greatest harms that a person can suffer": loss of life, loss of freedom, and grave bodily injury. (ibid.) If you advertise for someone who is willing to be killed and eaten, then the fact that I have answered your advert will not absolve you of culpability for homicide. In these cases *Volenti* must yield to a justified paternalism, in which persons are prevented from entering into agreements with others that will cause them serious harm.

Den Hartogh therefore concludes that the justification of euthanasia requires more than a fully informed and voluntary request by a decisionally capable person. The additional element is evidence of expected benefit, which is to be ensured by eligibility criteria requiring a serious and incurable medical condition that is causing unbearable suffering. The right to an assisted death therefore rests not on patient self-determination alone but on that element plus patient benefit.

The foregoing picture is quite coherent, but it looks rather different when we recognize that benefit has already been presupposed in the case for the right to suicide. In that case, both self-determination and benefit are in play throughout the argument, and the ethical gap between doing it yourself and enlisting assistance vanishes. Another way of putting the point is that it becomes necessary to rely on the *Volenti* principle only when the expected outcome of the involvement of the other is harm, rather than benefit. But that is not the case either for rational suicide or for euthanasia: both are intended to benefit, not harm. In that case, there is no *injuria* that *Volenti* needs to negative by means of consent. *Volenti* therefore need not be involved in the justification of a right to euthanasia, which can rest on the same values that ground a right to (rational) suicide.

As noted at the outset, the ethical justification for the intentional causing of death is strongest in the paradigmatic cases in which both self-determination and benefit are in play, as in both rational suicide and euthanasia. It is weaker when either is absent: either benefit without self-determination, as in the case of ending the lives of infants, or self-determination without benefit, as in the case of irrational suicide. Den Hartogh's ethical arguments, for both the right to suicide and the right to euthanasia, seem to presuppose the paradigm. In no case does self-determination appear to be working on its own.

Moral Methodology

If my conclusions are correct to this point, then they have implications for the argumentative strategy that Den Hartogh pursues throughout the book. He devotes a section of his Introduction to this matter of methodology, where he describes his arguments as "minimally revisionist". (p. 8) By this he means, in part, that he aims to start with widely shared convictions and then argue for principles that provide the best fit with those convictions. So far, this method is, as he says, "the usual one in bioethical discussions". But he also means something more specific, which points to a more distinctive feature of his methodology.

Den Hartogh observes that most writers who have sought to justify assisted dying have done so by denying that there is a morally relevant distinction either between doing and allowing, or between intending and foreseeing, or both. He correctly mentions me as one such. (ibid.) In my book-length treatment of assisted dying (Sumner 2011), I attempted to defend the practice by arguing from two already accepted practices in health care: the withdrawal of life-sustaining treatment and the administration of painkillers at levels likely to hasten death. These arguments required contending that, all other factors equal, there is no significant ethical difference between these practices and assisted dying. But assisted dying differs from withdrawing (or withholding) life-sustaining treatment by virtue of directly causing death rather than allowing it to happen as a result of natural causes, and it differs from administering large doses of painkillers by virtue of causing death intentionally rather than foreseeing it as an unavoidable side effect. So there could be no significant ethical difference between assisted dying and these accepted practices only if both the doing/allowing distinction and the intending/foreseeing distinction don't carry any ethical weight, at least in this context.

Den Hartogh is correct to contend that his argumentative strategy does not require him to reject either of these distinctions. So far, the claim of minimal revisionism seems well justified. However, at a closer look the differences between his strategy and mine tend to vanish. The key in both cases is the distinction between harm and benefit. I have already suggested that Den Hartogh's argumentative transition from the right to end one's own life to the right to enlist the assistance of others is eased by resting the former not merely on the right of self-determination but also on the implicit assumption that death will be a benefit. If one's suicide will instead be a harm—either to self or, especially, to others—it becomes difficult or impossible to shelter it under a right of self-determination.

The distinction between harm and benefit is equally crucial in my arguments. Traditional defences of the doing/allowing and intending/foreseeing distinctions argue that it is worse to cause someone harm than allow it to befall them, and worse to intend it rather than foresee it as a side effect. Whether these defences are successful is a matter of perennial ethical debate, especially between consequentialists and their opponents, but that debate is irrelevant to my argument because, like Den Hartogh, I was presupposing a context in which death is not a harm but a benefit. Where benefits rather than harms are concerned the traditional distinctions have much less bite; indeed, if anything, it is better to confer a benefit on someone than to merely allow it to accrue to them, and better to intend it than to merely foresee it as a side effect.

I therefore did not need to, and did not, deny the moral relevance of these distinctions, as usually understood in their usual context. Instead, I relied on the crucial fact that, in any context in which either suicide or euthanasia can be justified, death can be expected to be a benefit rather than a harm. Den Hartogh's argument also relies on this fact. Though it remains true that we each deploy our defence of assisting dying in our own particular way, at bottom the similarities between our methodologies are more significant than the differences. We can each claim, with some degree of credibility, that our argumentative strategy is minimally revisionist.

The Two Tracks

My comments to this point have neglected a significant further element in Den Hartogh's defence of assisted dying. Having had considerable experience within the Dutch euthanasia regime, he is, by and large, supportive of it. But only by and large. In some respects he prefers the system in place in Oregon, where qualified patients are given a prescription for lethal medication which they can ingest orally at the time and in the place of their choosing—or, as happens in a substantial minority of cases, not at all. In comparing the two regimes, what turns out to matter for Den Hartogh is life expectancy. The Dutch system, he says, works well for patients "in the last stage of a terminal illness", but not so well for those with "an indeterminate life expectancy". (2023, p. 327) With respect to this latter category, Den Hartogh primarily has in mind three groups of patients: the very elderly, who typically present with an accumulation of old-age ailments; those whose qualifying illness is solely, or primarily, mental, rather than physical; and persons in the early stages of dementia.[6]

Den Hartogh mentions four respects in which persons in these groups may satisfy the qualifying conditions for euthanasia less readily than those with a terminal illness: (1) it may be less clear that their request is fully voluntary; (2) they may be more ambivalent about dying when the further progression of their illness(es) remains uncertain; (3) their suffering may be more multidimensional and existential, and therefore more difficult to appreciate and assess; and (4) it may be more difficult to determine whether there are alternative ways of treating and alleviating that suffering. For these persons, Den Hartogh proposes something more like the Oregon model, where, in order to receive a prescription for life-ending medication, they would only need to convince two doctors that their request was "voluntary, well-informed, well-considered and stable." (p. 329) They would not need to provide any evidence of either a serious and incurable medical condition or unbearable suffering. In other words, they would not have to show that death would be a benefit for them.

Den Hartogh therefore advocates for (what he calls) a "dual-track" system: "a 'Dutch' arrangement for patients in the final stage of a fatal illness, and an 'Oregon' arrangement for people with an indeterminate life expectancy." (p. 331) For those on track one, euthanasia is justified by both patient self-determination and expected patient benefit, while for track two patients self-determination alone will suffice. Den Hartogh acknowledges that any dividing line between the two cohorts will inevitably be arbitrary. He is tempted to propose that, in order to qualify for track one, a patient must have a life expectancy of no more than six months,

---

6   As den Hartogh notes, in 2020 patients in these three groups jointly comprised 7% of all euthanasia cases in the Netherlands.

but he recognizes that these prognoses are often very unreliable. In the end, he settles for the vague requirement that the patient's death must be "reasonably foreseeable".

As Den Hartogh notes, that phrase and this qualifying condition originated in the Canadian assisted dying legislation that came into effect in June 2016.[7] However, in 2019 it was challenged in a Quebec court by two plaintiffs whose condition made it clear that, in order to be excluded by the "reasonably foreseeable natural death" condition, a patient need not belong to any of the three groups with which Den Hartogh was concerned.[8] Both plaintiffs had lifelong physical conditions that caused them great suffering but were not likely to be fatal anytime soon. At the time of the court hearing, Jean Truchon, 51, had had cerebral spastic paralysis with tripartism since birth, leaving him completely paralyzed except for the use of his left arm. Nicole Gladu, 73, had contracted an acute paralytic form of polio when she was four years old. At the age of 47 she was diagnosed with post-polio muscular degenerative syndrome, a progressive neurological disease characterized by generalized fatigue, muscle weakness, and muscle aches. Since that time she had also developed thrombophlebitis, hiatus hernia, severe osteoporosis, scoliosis of her spine, and pulmonary disease.

The court found that excluding the plaintiffs from eligibility for an assisted death on the sole ground that their natural deaths were not reasonably foreseeable violated their constitutionally guaranteed rights. When the federal government elected not to appeal this decision, recognizing that they would almost certainly lose, they accepted that they would need to amend the assisted dying legislation. That amendment, passed in April 2021, also created a dual-track system, but one that is very different from Den Hartogh's proposal.[9] For track one patients, whose expected deaths are sufficiently imminent, the eligibility conditions and safeguards remained essentially unchanged from the 2016 legislation. For those on the newly created track two, a number of additional procedures and safeguards were put in place to deal with the kinds of concerns that Den Hartogh has expressed, including: a longer waiting period between first assessment and provision (to ensure voluntariness and preclude ambivalence), a mandatory consultation with a specialist in the medical condition that is the basis of the assisted dying

---

7   *An Act to amend the Criminal Code and to make related amendments to other Acts (medical assistance in dying)*. 42nd Parl., 64-65 Elizabeth II, 2015-2016.
8   *Truchon c. Procureur général du Canada*, 2019 QCCS 3792.
9   *An Act to amend the Criminal Code (medical assistance in dying)*. 43rd Parl., 69-70 Elizabeth II, 2020-2021.

request (to explore other options for treating the condition), and discussion with the patient of other means available for relieving their suffering.

This dual-track regime, which remains in place in Canada, serves to illustrate how it is possible to respond to the same set of concerns in radically different ways. Both the Canadian government and Den Hartogh took the view that special problems would be presented by persons requesting an assisted death whose life expectancy is indeterminate. The government responded by adding further conditions to those already in place for track one patients. Den Hartogh's proposal, by contrast, was to remove eligibility conditions already in place for euthanasia, making it easier, not harder, for track two patients to access an assisted death. I find this deeply perplexing. If the worry is that there will be categories of persons seeking an assisted death — the very old, or patients with a mental illness or with mild dementia, or patients, like Truchon and Gladu, with serious but chronic physical illnesses — where the voluntariness or stability of their desire to die might be in question, or where there might remain some means of alleviating their condition, or where their suffering is too diffuse and existential to make for reliable assessment, then why would the appropriate response not be to add safeguards to track two designed to alleviate that worry? How can the best regime be one which makes it easier for everyone in these categories to end their own life by providing them with the means to do so, as long as their request is "voluntary, well-informed, well-considered and stable"?

However this may be, the fact remains that there is one component of Den Hartogh's ideal assisted dying regime that is grounded strictly in self-determination, with no requirement of expected patient benefit. However, to my mind at least, it is the least attractive one.

Last Words

In the foregoing, I have taken issue with some of the main themes in Govert Den Hartogh's book. In doing so I may have left the impression that I disagree with most of his contentions or that I have learned little from the book. If so, I wish to end by dispelling that impression.

This book is not a stand-alone effort. Instead, it brings together work that Den Hartogh has been doing on its various topics over the past two decades or so. The end-of-life literature is now massive (if you doubt this, just take a look at his list of works cited) and, as someone working in this field, I have had to economize by sorting out the contributors most worth reading. Den Hartogh is one of them and his virtues are on display in this book. Begin with the range of topics covered. I have said nothing about his treatment of palliative care, or of continuous deep sedation, or of stopping eating and drinking, or of advance directives, or of the Dutch and Belgian regulatory systems, or of conscientious objection, and very little about his extensive discussion of mental illness or the "completed life". Anyone wishing further enlightenment on any of those topics will be richly rewarded by reading this book.

I particularly appreciate four qualities in work in bioethics: clear, effective communication; careful, well-organized argumentation; thorough, comprehensive research; and responsiveness to empirical evidence. Den Hartogh delivers on all four, which is why I learned so much more from this book than my foregoing critique would indicate. When we philosophers comment on one another's work we are trained to target points of disagreement; for us, refutation is the sincerest form of flattery. The fact that I found some themes in the book with which to take issue should not obscure the fact that there is much more agreement between the two of us than disagreement. I have the highest regard for Den Hartogh's work and hope to continue learning from it.

About the author

L.W. Sumner (wayne.sumner@utoronto.ca) is Emeritus Professor in the University of Toronto's Department of Philosophy, with special interest in normative and applied ethics, political philosophy, and the philosophy of law.

Literature

Den Hartogh, Govert. *What Kind of Death. The Ethics of Determining One's Own Death*. New York: Routledge, 2023.
Hohfeld, Wesley Newcomb. *Fundamental Legal Conceptions as Applied in Judicial Reasoning*. Edited by Walter Wheeler Cook. New Haven and London: Yale University Press, 1919.
Mill, John Stuart. "On Liberty [1859]." In *Utilitarianism and on Liberty*, edited by Mary Warnock. Malden, MA: Blackwell Publishing, 2003.
Sumner, L.W. *Assisted Death: A Study in Ethics and Law*. Oxford: Oxford University Press, 2011.
Sumner, L.W. *The Moral Foundation of Rights*. Oxford: Clarendon Press, 1987.

Whose Life is it Anyway? Some Reflections on Den Hartogh's *What Kind of Death*

Thomas Mertens

Abstract

This contribution will restrict itself to Den Hartogh's conceptual framework and formulate some hesitations about Den Hartogh's moral premises which he calls 'ethical atoms' (p. 159-160, 317). For at least two reasons I will discuss these premises with a certain reluctance. First of all, the sensitive nature of what is at stake here: matters of life and death and the question of what we owe others and ourselves; secondly and more on a more personal level, my hesitations do not lead to any clear alternative moral premises. Especially with regard to Den Hartogh's central premiss concerning self-determination, I sympathise Velleman's approach in one of his famous articles: I am neither completely pro nor completely con. I am more, like, not so sure.

Keywords: right to self-determination, right to life, right to die, right to private life, 'Volenti non fit iniuria'.

Introduction

Den Hartogh's *What Kind of Death* is a very interesting and rich book, and it will definitively become one of the works to consult when discussing (conceptual) issues such as (assisted) suicide, euthanasia, the right to life and the right to self-determination. At the same time, it is empirically rich and well-informed – it will be of use when devising legal regimes that will govern euthanasia in relation to mental illnesses, old age, and advance

---

Gijs van Donselaar, Peter Rijpkema, and Henri Wijsbek (eds), *The Ethics of Determining One's Own Death. Essays on Den Hartogh's What Kind of Death.*
Taylor & Francis Group, 2025
DOI: https://doi.org/10.5117/FEP2024.1.004.MERT

directives. It starts out with a few well-defined moral premisses, but it doesn't shy away from discussing hard cases and from suggesting how to deal with those cases.

The Right to Self-Determination

Even before starting to study Den Hartogh's monograph, it becomes evident what his moral premiss or 'ethical axiom' is. Just have a look at the subtitle of his book: "The Ethics of Determining One's Own Death". Apparently, this book is based on the view that everyone is entitled to determine (the moment of) his or her own death. The moral question arises 'merely' with regard to the 'how' and the 'when' to bring about one's own death, not with regard to the 'whether' one has such a right. Contrary to centuries of religious and non-religious thinking in which the ending of one's life at one's own hand was seen as a sin, as a crime or as a most deplorable event, Den Hartogh is convinced that everyone has in principle the right to end one's life (although some cases of suicide obviously remain deplorable also in his view).

The impression given by the sub-title that only the 'how' and the 'when' are at stake here, is confirmed by the book's table of contents. It first discusses the issue of suicide and argues that ending one's own life at one's own doing can be a rational and well considered decision. Only thereafter the question is considered as to how and under which conditions another person can assist the self in bringing about his or her death. In this sense this is not primarily a monograph on euthanasia, because the legitimacy of other persons, including medical doctors, in assisting the self to die and the manners in which this may be done, is derived from and depending on this first premiss: as part of the right to self-determination, it is within the domain of every human being to end his or her life,

The book's introduction confirms Den Hartogh's moral point of departure straight away. Here it is stated clearly that people have a right to decide about the manner and time of their death. Such a decision belongs to the "core of self-regarding choices": each person is "authorised" to make for himself or herself this decision, provided such a decision is made "without undue pressure and after due reflection" or, formulated differently, is "voluntary and competently made". (p. 5, 31) This moral premiss contains at least two elements, namely the idea of human self-determination and a specific understanding of the right to life. Obviously, there is also the question whether suicide can ever be truly understood as an expression of self-determination. I will come back briefly to this issue at the end of this paper.

It is rather surprising that Den Hartogh refers repeatedly to the (concept of the) right to self-determination, but gives us little by way of justifying his extensive view of self-determination. Maybe this is what an 'ethical atom' implies. The right is described as a "bundle of normative assets" (p. 29) that carve out a private domain in which an individual is entitled to decide for himself or herself what to do with one's life and how to live and how to die. Since self-determination is presumed to be a fundamental right, other people have corresponding duties, i.e., not to interfere with these decisions, irrespective of the content of these decisions. Each and every individual is 'sovereign' with regard to how he or she organises his of her life, because this expresses this person's autonomy and because others cannot decide what is best for another person. (p. 29-30)

Obviously, the right to organise one's own life, is not unlimited. As soon as one's decision concerning one's (own) life harms or threatens to harm the interests of others, the limits of one's personal sovereignty are reached. This is one of the fundamentals of liberal thought that we can even find in Kant: "any action is right if it can coexist with everyone's freedom in accordance with a universal law". The right to self-determination thus means that you are entitled to make your own decisions regarding your own life, as long as these decisions are compatible with the same right to self-determination of others. According to Den Hartogh, the right to decide to end one's own life – if this decision is reached, as already said, without undue pressure and after due reflection (p. 5) – forms part of the right to self-determination (p. 31, 34, 51) and is in principle self-regarding.

The Right to Life

A crucial step within Den Hartogh's thinking is the following: since the right to self-determination encompasses the right to die, he must defend a particular understanding of the right to life. This right, Den Hartogh writes, not only serves a person's interest in survival, but also empowers a person to end his or her life. Life is conceived as what is "most essentially yours". If you were not really "the owner of your life", then to end your life is not a decision for you to make. You are then at best merely a "trustee". (p. 31) The view that 'life' belongs to the person who lives this live, is certainly not self-evident. Again, centuries of religious and non-religious thinking have denied that your life is your property or that the right to die exists. Neither is Den Hartogh's view in line with the right to life as laid down in important human rights documents, such as the European Convention of Human Rights.

This important legal document holds a much more limited view on the right to life. It is true that the Convention mentions this right as the first of its list of fundamental rights, and thus regards it as of high importance, but it does not imply 'ownership' of the person who lives his or her life. Article 2 of the Convention reads as follows: "Everyone's right to life shall be protected by law. No one shall be deprived of his life intentionally". Both elements, the protection of the (right to) life and the prohibition of the deliberate taking of life, underline the important value of life. Its importance can only be set aside when other important values overrule the importance of life. Articles 2 enumerates four such values that may – under particular and strict conditions – be considered as more important than life. The first of these values is a particular form of punishment. The right to life did not – at the time the Convention was established – exclude the death penalty. The idea was, of course, that a person who took the life of another person, had forfeited his (or her) right to life. Since then, a later protocol to the Convention has abolished the death penalty within the realm of the Council of Europe as incompatible with the right to life. The three other values that may overrule the value of life and are still in place, arise in the following three situations: someone gets killed while (unlawfully) threatening the life of another person or persons; someone gets killed in an attempt to arrest him (or her) or in an attempt to escape detention; someone gets killed in the process of suppressing an uprising or riot. If the use of lethal force in these cases is both "necessary and proportionate", the killing of the person(s) is not a violation of their right to life.

It is important to understand what this implies for Article 2's view on the right to life. Firstly, what matters predominantly in this right is the protection of human life. This is what the law ought to do. The exceptions mentioned solely revolve around situations in which the state is legitimized to take life and is, so to speak, freed from its duty to protect life. Obviously, the formulation of ECHR does not exclude cases of interpersonal legitimate self-defence, although the state has the duty to investigate these cases. Clearly, the addressee of the right to life in ECHR is the state, not the subjects (or citizens) of that legal order. It tells the state what to do and what not. The reason why the death penalty is included in the first paragraph (of Article 2) and the other exceptions in its second paragraph, is the direct or (merely) indirect intention of the state of killing in order to uphold values considered more important than (the protection of) life: directly in the case of criminal law, indirectly in the case of the values of protecting innocent life, making lawful arrests and upholding (or restoring) public order. It is clear that Article 2 does not entail a subjective right to end one's own life. It does not explicitly prohibit the taking of one's own life, but it would follow from the state's duty to protect life that the state should aim at preventing suicide and should prohibit assisted suicide. In the well-known Pretty-case, discussed by Den Hartogh (p. 159), the European court stated that the right to life could not without a distortion of language be interpreted as conferring a diametrically opposed right, namely a right to die.

Obviously, one can argue that a formulation and an interpretation of the right to life by and on the basis of a legal document such as the European Convention does not decide on the moral meaning of the right to life. It may indeed be the case that Article 2 sees the right to life primarily as a vertical relationship between particular states and their citizens and that the states have given (in the Convention) the right to life a too limited scope. Positive law is not decisive for a moral understanding of this right. Morally speaking, 'bearers' of the right to life should be authorized to decide whether they want to continue to live or not. Already in the Pretty-case, the Court stated, as Den Hartogh mentions (p. 32), that the law preventing her (Pretty) to exercise her choice (to die) might be an interference with her right to respect for private life.

When bringing the right to life and to die within the orbit of the right to self-determination, Den Hartogh seems to place himself within a (particular) natural law understanding of human rights. He accepts the view that humans have certain rights simply by their nature. He apparently rejects an alternative, more positivist understanding of these rights such as the one defended by philosophers like Bentham and Kelsen (and maybe even by Kant). They argue that every 'subjective' right must be viewed as a child of 'objective' law. There are no subjective rights that 'exist' prior to a particular legal order. According to this reading, conventions or treaties of human rights are constitutive of these rights and not (merely) declarative. Fortunately for Den Hartogh, bringing the right to life as including a right to die within the orbit of the right to self-determination does not need to rely only on (a liberal interpretation of) natural law.

Positive law has moved into that direction as well, albeit not in the context of the right to life. In recent years, the European Court of Human Rights has decided that humans have the right to choose their own death, not on the basis of the Convention's right to life, but on the basis of its right to private life as formulated in Article 8. In the well-known Haas-decision the Court decided that this Article implies "the right to determine the manner and time of one's own death", as mentioned by Den Hartogh. (p. 32) In its judgment, however, the Court does not spell out how it understands the relationship between Article 8 and Article 2: must the right to die as part of the right to private life be understood as independent of the right to life? The Court merely states that the Convention must be read as a whole. It does not address, nor does Den Hartogh, the suggestion that Article 8 can take priority over Article 2 with regard to decisions concerning the end of life. Should one perhaps understand the right to private life as an amendment to the right to life, in the sense that it is no longer the duty of the state to protect the life of those who 'voluntary and competently' make the decision to end their lives? Or should one consider the right to life as irrelevant with regard to decisions concerning the (voluntary) ending of one's own life? In any case, Den Hartogh seems to support this line of reasoning which has recently also been endorsed in an important decision by the German Constitutional Court. On the basis of the German Constitution's commitment to human dignity and to the general right of personality, this court decided that indeed the right to a self-determined death exists.

The Volenti-principle

If my life is mine in the sense that I have the right to end it, the question arises whether I can transfer my right to life to someone else. In other words: if the right to self-determination includes the right to determine the manner and the time of one's death, does it also include the right to authorise someone else to execute my death wish or assist me with executing my decision? This would seem to be the case: it is not only difficult to execute one's decision to die, but for some persons it is simply impossible. Can this decision therefore be delegated or transferred to others? In principle, the German Constitutional Court gives an affirmative answer here: the right to self-determination (to decide on the end of one's life) implies the freedom to seek and utilise assistance from third parties (Para. 212). According to this court, there is no strict separation or barrier between one's decision to exercise one's right to die and one's decision to seek and obtain the assistance of someone else in order to bring about death. If 'assisted suicide services' would be criminalized, the right to suicide would in certain constellations be effectively vitiated (Para. 264).

If I understand Den Hartogh correctly, he is much more hesitant here. He repeatedly confirms the importance of the right of self-determination and the right to end one's own life, but he also repeatedly adds an important caveat. Nowhere does he describe the relationship between 'self' and 'life' as one of property holder and property, as one would perhaps expect. Den Hartogh's vocabulary is more cautious: "you are the owner of your own life"; "our lives belong to the core of our personal domain" (p. 31, 155, 169). This cautiousness comes out most clearly when Den Hartogh discusses the so-called Volenti-principle which says that no injury, no wrong is done to a consenting person (*'volenti non fit iniuria'*).

This principle can be illustrated by a very basic example: when a person gets punched on the nose during a boxing match in which he voluntary participates, he is clearly hurt but he is not wronged. Since he consented to participate in this match, he accepted the risks involved in this sport. Den Hartogh mentions this principle several times and describes it as a principle which governs in particular tort law: one cannot be wronged by an action to which one has consented (p. 8, 83, 157, 172). But he consistently rejects the Volenti-principle as "a general moral principle that covers all actions." In particular he states that this principle does not apply to basic human rights that are considered "inalienable", such as the right to bodily integrity, to personal freedom and to life. There exists, he writes, a small subset of human rights (bodily integrity, personal freedom, life) that are "traditionally held to be inalienable" (p. 156). Den Hartogh agrees with this tradition: these rights are indeed "unwaivable" (p 83). In other words, even if one consents to being corporally maimed, to becoming a slave or to giving away or transferring one's life, one would still be wronged.

The reasons why Den Hartogh rejects the Volenti-principle as a general moral principle, do not become fully clear. He refers to the fact that no legal system accepts consent as a justification for killing (p. 8) and that it merely functions as a manner of shielding the other party from liability. (p. 172) However, the fact that legal systems *de facto* accept this principle only as a limited one and that certain basic rights are widely considered as inalienable, is not sufficient as a moral argument. Den Hartogh mentions that Feinberg, not an unimportant voice in the debate on the right to life, argues in favour of applying Volenti without exceptions in criminal and in tort law. (p. 157) Likewise, commonsense morality would, according to Den Hartogh, also be in favour of extending the applicability of Volenti-principle. (p. 7) Contrary to this view, Den Hartogh defends that the right to self-determination includes the right to die at one's own doing, but not the right to transfer the right to die to someone else.

Would it not have been more consistent if Den Hartogh had sided with Feinberg and commonsense morality? If the right to self-determination includes the right to die, why would it not be permissible to transfer the decision to die to someone else, provided the decision is made "without undue pressure and after due reflection" and that no other person is duty-bound to provide such assistance? But this is not Den Hartogh's view. Even though the right to life belongs to the person who lives this life, Den Hartogh defends that the right to life, together with the right to bodily integrity and personal freedom, is unwaivable and cannot be transferred (pp. 5-6; p. 83, 156). A person's life can only be ended by someone else when that person has freely ("without undue pressure and after due reflection") decided to end his or her life and it is in that person's interest to have his or her life ended. (p. 6) This view comes at a price. Apparently, the right to self-determination is a necessary and a sufficient condition only for ending one's own life. In cases in which others are involved, consent (self-determination) is necessary but not enough. If the interest of the person who decides to die, must be taken into consideration by the person whose assistance is required, an element of paternalism necessarily enters into the discussion. Den Hartogh acknowledges this but defends that certain paternalism accusations (p. 8, primarily that it infringes personal sovereignty, p. 169) are mistaken and that there is nothing objectionable to indirect paternalism.

In my view, any form of paternalism, direct or indirect, sits unconformably with self-determination. It forces Den Hartogh to defend human rights on the basis of an interest-theory rather than the choice-theory. (p. 29, 156) The idea that human rights protect choices rather than interests would fit much better with self-determination as the supreme value. Den Hartogh's rejection of the Volenti-principle as a general moral principle (based on choice and consent) is most prominently formulated as follows: "it is not contradictory to permit you to cause harm to yourself by doing something, but not to permit anyone else to cause similar harm to you on your request". (p. 83) In other words, despite the fact that I am the owner of my life, despite the fact that my life is my domain and despite the fact that I have the right to end my life, I do not have the right to let someone else do the active ending for me. Why is this not contradictory? Perhaps the answer lies in the following consideration. Den Hartogh describes the relationship between 'self' and 'life' as one of (self-)determination, but he does not fully consider, as he perhaps should have done, 'life' as the property of the person who lives the life. Nowhere does Den Hartogh calls 'life' the property of the person who lives the life. Apparently for him there is a difference between me being the owner of my life (p. 31) and me considering my life as my property.

My life as my Property?

The idea that I am not the proprietor of my life is a classic idea that often stands at the basis of moral and legal condemnations of suicide. Kant defends the view that humans are, with regard to their own life and body, '*sui iuris*' but not '*sui dominus*'. Human beings are self-determining beings, in the sense that they ought – and are able – to lead a moral life, but they are not the proprietors of themselves.

Kant presents us with two arguments: being the proprietor of oneself would be contradictory, for as a person he or she would be a subject that can hold property and as something that is owned, he or she should be considered a thing. It is impossible to be proprietor and property, person and thing, at the same time. Although this argument draws on Kant's well-known, but perhaps not fully rigid, distinction between persons and things, it also resonates with the view that nobody's existence is his or her own creation. In that sense everybody's 'self' is a 'given', or – perhaps in a better formulation – a 'Geworfenheit' to use Heidegger's idiom. That's why the idea of self-determination should, in my view, not be given a predominant, let alone an exclusive, place in discussions on life and death.

Kant's second argument is related but slightly different. If something is one's property, Kant writes, one can *in principle* do with it whatever one likes (unless the rights of others are at stake which is obviously the case most of the time). Humans, however, cannot treat themselves in whatever way they like since they have obligations towards themselves. They are accountable to humanity in their own person, says Kant. Nowadays, the idea that humans have duties to themselves is not a popular one and Den Hartogh does not seem to consider the right to self-determination as a source of obligations that one owes oneself.

Finally, make no mistake. Kant's arguments against self-ownership do not imply a categorical prohibition of suicide. Suicide for prudential reasons is according to Kant strictly prohibited (many 'Kantians' doubt whether this is correct), but he acknowledges the possibility of what is sometimes called altruistic suicide. These are forms of sacrifice of the self in order to promote morality or to safeguard moral standing. These are cases, in which one's life is threatened by death and where life can only be saved by giving up of one's moral standing. One simple example Kant mentions is that of a Scottish rebel who was offered the choice between death and convict labor: "a man of honor would choose death and only the scoundrel convict labor". Perhaps this is for us not the most convincing example, but it shows that for Kant, biological life itself is not the highest value. Elsewhere he mentions a soldier who chooses a certain death to save his country; a political leader who is willing to consume a fast-acting poison in order not to be captured by the enemy; a person who decides to be vaccinated and therewith puts himself in mortal danger. Perhaps these cases of (risking) suicide, to which

Den Hartogh adds a few more contemporary and more fitting examples (p. 57), can perhaps be understood as an expression of self-determination but only in the sense that the self is dedicated to aims that transcend the 'self'.

About the author

Thomas Mertens (Thomas.mertens@ru.nl), emeritus professor of law at the Radboud University Nijmegen, is a specialist on the relationship between law and morality. He has published extensively on human rights, Kant's moral and legal philosophy, and on law and morality in Nazi-Germany.

Literature

Feinberg, J. "Voluntary Euthanasia and the Inalienable Right to Life", *Philosophy & Public Affairs* 7 (1978) 93-123.

Den Hartogh, G. *What Kind of Death. The Ethics of Determining One's Own Death.* New York/London: Routledge, 2023.

Den Hartogh, G. "Decriminalising Assisted Suicide Services" (case note), *European Constitutional Law Review* 16 (2020) 713-732.

Mertens, Th. "Kant and the ends of life", in: D. Dall'Agnol (ed.), *Kantian Perspectives in Bioethics,* Pisa: Edizioni ETS, 2015, 33-52.

Kant, I. *Die Metaphysik der Sitten*, Akademie Ausgabe Band VI, Berlin: De Gruyter, 1901.

Urteil des Bundesverfassungsgerichts, 2BvR 2347/15; 651/16; 1261/16; 2354/16; 2527/16 (20 Februar 2020).

J.D. Velleman, J.D. "A Right to Self-Termination", *Ethics* 109 (1999) 606-628.

Dual or Single Gauge? Govert den Hartogh's 'Dual-Track' Assisted Death

Isra Black[1]

Abstract

In *What Kind of Death: The Ethics of Determining One's Own Death* (2023), Govert den Hartogh offers a 'dual-track' model for assisted death. According to Den Hartogh's model, mere access to lethal drugs would be lawful on the basis of an autonomous decision (Track 1), while "full-blown physician-assisted death" (provision of lethal means under professional supervision and care) would be lawful in the presence of an autonomous decision and satisfaction of further conditions instantiating values including dignity and well-being (Track 2). I offer a critical reading of Den Hartogh's argument in respect of the nature and justification of Track 1. I argue that permitting mere access to lethal medication may be both "lifting a blockade" (as Den Hartogh argues) and assisting an individual to die (as he denies). This conclusion about the *nature* of Track 1 opens the question of the sufficiency of Den Hartogh's claim that autonomy is its sole normative ground. A revised account of the *justification* for Track 1 is possible, however. I argue that Track 1 assistance may be permissible on the same grounds as Den Hartogh provides for Track 2: autonomy in conjunction with other values (albeit in a different mix). Rather than conceive of Den Hartogh's model for assisted death as 'dual-track', dual gauge, we might rather consider mere access to lethal drugs and full-blown physician assisted death as two services on a single normative gauge.

Keywords: assisted death; assisted dying; assisted suicide; euthanasia; Govert den Hartogh.

---

1   I am grateful to Gijs van Donselaar, Lisa Forsberg, and Henri Wijsbek for feedback and suggestions on earlier versions of this article. I would also like to thank the organisers (Peter Rijpkema and Gijs van Donselaar) and participants of the 'Ethics of End-of-Life Decisions' conference at UvA Amsterdam Law School in September 2023, as well as Govert den Hartogh for his generous response to the presentation on which this article is based.

Gijs van Donselaar, Peter Rijpkema, and Henri Wijsbek (eds), *The Ethics of Determining One's Own Death. Essays on Den Hartogh's What Kind of Death.*
Taylor & Francis Group, 2025
DOI: https://doi.org/10.5117/FEP2024.1.005.BLAC

Introduction

Govert den Hartogh's monograph, *What Kind of Death: The Ethics of Determining One's Own Death* (2023), offers a rich seam of integrated thought on the ethics — and regulation — of end-of-life decisions and interventions, including suicide, stopping eating and drinking, suffering, advance decisions (or directives), palliative care, continuous and terminal sedation, as well as assisted suicide and voluntary euthanasia. Den Hartogh offers insights across these topics; his contributions merit wide reading and broad discussion.

Thus it is with some diffidence that my focus in this article is assisted death—an umbrella term for assisted suicide and voluntary euthanasia.[2] So to do risks neglecting the unity of *What Kind of Death* or unduly downplaying the significance of the book's other parts. Nevertheless, I shall attend to assisted death because of the interest and innovation that lie in Den Hartogh's 'dual-track' model (or schema) for access to life-ending means.

According to Den Hartogh's 'dual-track' model, the respective tracks — (mere) access to lethal drugs (for example, mere prescription of a fatal dose of barbiturates by a physician) and access to 'full-blown' physician-assisted death (*viz*, provision of lethal means under professional supervision and care) — might co-exist as regulatory responses to the individual's interest in deciding (or wish to decide) the manner and moment of death within a single jurisdiction. On Den Hartogh's view, these two tracks are different in the nature, since mere access to lethal drugs (which I shall often call 'Track 1') does not involve assistance to die, unlike full-blown physician-assisted death (which I shall often call 'Track 2'). Further, Tracks 1 and 2 have eligibility criteria that reflect distinct and differently stringent normative underpinnings — mere access to lethal drugs takes support from the value of autonomy (or self-determination) alone, while autonomy together with other goods (such as dignity and well-being) ground full-blown physician-assisted death. To wit, within a dual-track regime there would be broad access to (safe) lethal medication and narrower access to full-blown physician assistance.

---

2 Some definitions. A person (P) performs suicide iff a) P follows a course of conduct (φ) that causes their own death; and b) P intends that their death obtains by means of φ. I shall broach suicide assistance later on. A third party (T) performs euthanasia on P iff a) T deliberately (and proximately) causes P's death; and b) death is good for P. Euthanasia is *voluntary* when P consents to T causing P's death; it is *involuntary* when P refuses consent to T causing P's death; it is *non-voluntary* when P is presently unable to consent to T causing P's death and P has neither consented to nor refused euthanasia in the past such that it would be voluntary or involuntary, respectively.

Den Hartogh's dual-track model innovates insofar as, to my knowledge, no jurisdiction has made provision for co-existing *permissive* regimes for access to life-ending means, where access to lethal medication is common to both limbs of the institutional framework and the limbs' substantive eligibility criteria follow the underpinnings detailed above. Further, Den Hartogh's dual-track model has normative attractions, since it extends the prospect of a minimally 'good' death to all autonomous individuals, that is, beyond the class(es) of individuals often thought the most appropriate candidates for full-blown physician-assisted death (self-determining agents with either terminal illness or unbearable, persistent, and unrelievable suffering). As such, the dual-track model may offer a solution to the problems (and potential injustices) in denying *any* access to life-ending means in so-called 'hard cases' (or perhaps better: for 'hard classes'): individuals who suffer with refractory mental disorders or who are 'tired of life'.

I am friendly to Den Hartogh's dual-track model. However, in what follows—and after further elaboration of the model in the next section—I would like to apply critical pressure to the account that Den Hartogh gives for Track 1. I shall advance two main lines of argument. First, I argue against Den Hartogh's claim that when an agent deblocks another's access to lethal medication, the former does not assist the latter to die. Second, Den Hartogh rests the justification for Track 1 on the value of self-determination alone. I argue that setting autonomous agency as the sole exercise condition for Track 1 need not entail that self-determination is the sole value that justifies mere access to lethal medication; other values may be in play. These arguments yield the conclusion that the nature and justification of Track 1 is not unlike that of Track 2 for full blown physician-assisted death. Rather than two tracks for assisted death of distinct normative gauge, we might instead think of mere access to lethal drugs and access to full-blown physician-assisted death as two services on a single gauge.

Den Hartogh's dual-track model for access to life-ending means

For accessibility of the argument that follows and so readers may avoid constant reference to *What Kind of Death*, I shall attempt to précis Den Hartogh's dual-track model. I first outline Track 1, then Track 2.

Track 1: Mere access to lethal drugs
Den Hartogh argues that individuals possess a right to decide how and when to die (pp. 28-34). (Elsewhere — discussing refusals of life-prolonging

medical treatment — I style this right as 'right *D*' (Black 2018); I adopt the shorthand here.) Right *D* is underpinned by the value of autonomy;[3] it is "most plausibly considered an element of the right to self-determination", that is, the:

> bundle of normative assets that together delineate a private domain within which it is up to you to decide what you do. You are not only free to make these decisions, you also have the authority to make them (p. 29; see Mackenzie 2008).

On Den Hartogh's view, an autonomy-derived right *D* grounds a content-independent duty on others not to interfere in the execution of one's life (or death) plans. That is, others' duty to respect the right is not a function of the "prudential or moral quality" of one's decision-making (p. 29). Den Hartogh offers a variety of reasons for content-independence. First, we might say that "the area of private sovereignty" enabled by the right to self-determination is intrinsically valuable (or has value in itself) (p. 30). Den Hartogh holds that autonomy is "in itself an essential element of a good life" (p. 30; see Hurka 1987). Second, we might hold that autonomy is instrumentally valuable (or has value as a means to some end). Den Hartogh argues that a right to carve out an area of private sovereignty has value "because of the social status it implies, of being an equal among equals" (p. 30). Here, it is the contribution of autonomy to status or equality that supports content-independence (see Nagel 1995). Third, a content-independent duty of non-interference with right *D* may arise for epistemic reasons (see Atkins 2000; Black 2018), *viz*, the individual occupying a privileged position in respect of knowledge of their own good vis-à-vis other actors. Epistemic deference may be instrumentally valuable. As Den Hartogh observes, "allowing people to act on their own ideal of the good death [including suicide] may increase their opportunities to come closer to it" compared to the situation in which others set the parameters for the manner and moment of death (p. 30).

I should emphasise that Den Hartogh takes care to avoid the implausible view that right *D* grounds an *unlimited* content-independent duty of non-interference on others: "the authority, assigned by a right, need not be

---

3   It follows that the conditions for the exercise of autonomy apply to the exercise of right *D*, *viz*, decision-making capacity and voluntariness (Den Hartogh 2023, p. 31; Black 2018, pp. 37-38). We might further add that in order for an agent to take an autonomous decision, their decision must be sufficiently informed. However, I take it on a decision-specific conception of capacity, an agent with capacity has sufficient grasp of the information relative to the decision. It is not necessary, therefore, to insist on a distinct sufficient information condition for autonomy.

unlimited" (p. 30). Rather, Den Hartogh's position is that one has *pro tanto* unlimited autonomy rights — including right D — but one's *all things considered* autonomy rights depend on the interaction of self-determination with other valuable features of the moral or political constellation: "the default is always that you are free to do what you want, and there have to be good reasons for restricting that freedom" (p. 30). As Joseph Raz writes:

> Rights are (part of) the justification of many duties. They justify the view that people have those duties. But… only to the extent that there are no conflicting considerations of greater weight (1986, p. 172).

Thus we might say that our all things considered rights are just those that persist after specification (Richardson 1990), because the relevant interests are sufficiently important to generate duties (Raz 1986, p. 166). We hold right D (and others have a content-independent duty of non-interference) just when the interest in deciding the manner and moment of death outcompetes (or survives conflict with) the rights of others. Den Hartogh would add that the right must also be compatible with "basic moral considerations, for example about human dignity, that cannot be cashed out in terms of human rights" (p. 31).

In light of the above, how — on Den Hartogh's view — might one specify a right of mere access to lethal medication (Track 1) out of the value of self-determination alone? Central to Den Hartogh's account is the claim that supply of fatal drugs when an individual satisfies the conditions for the exercise of autonomy merely amounts to discharge of the duty of non-interference with right D. I outline the argument in stages. First, there often exist market restrictions on lethal medication (p. 81). Second, such restrictions are generally, but not universally, well-founded. As Den Hartogh observes, "[lethal medication] can be used impulsively [for] suicides that cannot be regarded to be well-considered, or fully voluntary. In addition, they can be used for killing others" (p. 81). Third, in cases in which an individual has an autonomous wish to die, the reasons for restricting access to lethal medication do not apply: the agent has capacity and acts voluntarily (p. 81-82). Fourth, in such circumstances, granting access to lethal drugs is not an act of assistance to die but rather and merely amounts to "lifting a blockade" (p. 82). It is this purported fact of non-assistance that situates the individual's wish to die within their private domain, thereby giving rise to a content-independent duty of non-interference on others.

I shall say more on this argument shortly. However, I need first to outline Den Hartogh's argument for track 2 — full-blown physician-assisted death.

Track 2: 'Full-blown' physician-assisted death

Den Hartogh defines 'euthanasia' — what I describe as 'full-blown physician-assisted death' — as a "joint action" of the individual who wishes to die and a physician who takes "final responsibility for assuring that [the former] dies swiftly, safely and without pain" (p. 155-156). Euthanasia on Den Hartogh's usage, therefore, covers both instances of voluntary euthanasia *stricto sensu* and assisted suicide just when a physician is a co-participant in the relevant course of conduct. (As contrasted to the situation Den Hartogh foresees on Track 1, in which a physician might merely assess whether an individual is autonomous and prescribe lethal medication on this basis (p. 89).) I shall keep to full-blown physician-assisted death. Nothing substantive hangs on the difference in terminology between Den Hartogh and me.[4]

It is the physician's status as a co-participant in a life-ending course of conduct — as a joint agent — that distinguishes the permissibility conditions of Track 2 from those of Track 1. While, on Den Hartogh's view, the value of self-determination alone justifies mere access to lethal medication, autonomy "is only a necessary, not a sufficient condition" for full-blown physician assisted death (p. 156; cf. Raz 2013). As we shall see, the presence of other values is an individually necessary and jointly sufficient condition for the permissibility of Track 2 assistance to die. Why is this so? To pose the question:

> If we have the authority to decide to do something, correlated to other people's duty not to interfere, do we then not also have the authority to consent to someone else doing it, or cooperating with us in doing it? (p. 155)

Den Hartogh offers a detailed explanation for why one's agential authority alone does not license another's ending (or participation in ending) of one's own life, which I can only summarise here. To pick out two central aspects of the discussion: first, some (though — importantly — not all) instances of assisted death may be incompatible with the value of dignity, and second, refusal of assistance to die when one believes death would be a harm need not amount to impermissible paternalism.

In respect of dignity, Den Hartogh emphasises two dimensions of the value: the *buck-passing* and the *qualification*, respectively. On the buck-passing dimension, dignity is a "placeholder" for the set of reasons that

---

[4] As Den Hartogh acknowledges, his extension of euthanasia is a matter of "convenience... That there is no basic moral difference between euthanasia proper and suicide assistance of the full-blooded kind is not a conceptual truth" (p. 90).

require us "to treat people in certain ways, for example to honour their rights" (p. 163). One's dignity comprises the contents of those reasons, including those the value of autonomy gives. However, one's dignity is not only these reasons, insofar as the qualification dimension mandates in addition "a certain emotional disposition, an attitude of respect" (p. 163). It is this attitude of respect that stands in the way of some instances of assisted death, autonomy notwithstanding. For example, Den Hartogh cites cases in which the individual's wish to die indicates a "basic lack of self-respect" such that the provision of assistance seems impermissibly confirmatory (p. 166).[5]

Importantly, Den Hartogh argues that respect may not be the sole moral emotion required in response to the reasons constitutive of a person's moral status; sometimes, what is called for is care (p. 166). To wit, "on a correct understanding of the concept of dignity, the proper concern for a person's welfare should not be considered a response to her dignity but to her needs" (p. 166). It follows that some instances of physician-assisted death are compatible with human dignity, just when the provision of assistance exemplifies appropriate care for the interests and rights of the individual who dies:

> A doctor who would grant a patient's request for euthanasia merely because it has been competently made would be lacking in proper concern for that patient. Perhaps he would even be lacking in proper respect. But a doctor, who grants the request because he reasonably considers it to be in the patient's true interest to do so, cannot be accused of violating that patient's dignity (p. 167).

In respect of paternalism, we should first clarify what we mean by the term. As an initial definition, let us say that an act is paternalistic just when "the act in question constitutes an attempt to substitute one person's judgment [sic] for another's, to promote the latter's benefit" (Dworkin 1988, p. 123). Further, the judgement subject to interference must be that of an autonomous agent (p. 123). Next, it is helpful to identify the distinction between direct (pure) and indirect (impure) paternalism. As Den Hartogh writes:

---

5   "A psychiatrist told me that a man with a personality disorder once came to him requesting euthanasia, saying 'I am a plague to humanity, I am wrecking the lives of everyone around me'. In a file concerning another psychiatric patient the following disturbing explanation of her request is given: 'The patient indicated that she had had a life without love and therefore had no right to exist'" (p. 166).

Direct paternalism is a two-place relation: A interferes in the execution of B's plans in order to prevent harm to B. Indirect paternalism is a three-place relation: A interferes in the execution of B's plans in order to prevent harm to C, even though C has consented to B's actions (Den Hartogh 2023, p. 157).

Plausibly, legal restrictions on physician-assisted death in jurisdictions where the practice is lawful are indirectly paternalistic. The State criminalises (or otherwise sanctions) physicians who assist autonomous individuals to die unless, *inter alia*, another substantive criterion (for example, going to the nature and degree of suffering) is also met. One way to explain the presence of this additional criterion is that its purpose is to avert harm to (or to promote the good of) individuals whose autonomous wishes to die will go unfulfilled as a result (see Kamm 1999; Sumner 2011; Black 2021). Let us grant that restrictions on the permissibility of physician-assisted death amount to indirect paternalism. Would this unsettle the foundations of Den Hartogh's Track 2 physician-assisted death? Only if it is true that paternalism is wrongful in this context. Den Hartogh considers two general objections — drawn from Feinberg (1986) — to paternalism that may seem to support a right to physician-assisted death on the basis of self-determination alone: the 'self-governance' objection and the 'status' objection. Neither succeed, for the reasons given below.

On the self-governance objection, it might be thought an affront or an 'insult' to an agent's autonomy to fail to lend a hand in their projects (p. 169). However, this misidentifies where the value in self-determination is realised. Even if autonomy is instantiated on achievement of one's ends, one is also self-governing when "allowed to set and pursue [one's] aims with the means at [one's] disposal" (p. 170). Consider an individual who campaigns — perhaps against the tide of public opinion and support — for some cause, never to see it widely realised during their lifetime (or maybe at all); we would not deny that their life was one of self-direction, notwithstanding the absence of success. Likewise, it seems a mistake to hold that an individual is denied self-governance when their wish for physician-assisted death on the mere basis of autonomy goes unfulfilled. The end of death remains their own to hold, but this particular means is not theirs alone.

It seems, then, that the self-governance objection to paternalism in the context of Track 2 is not really in play. As Den Hartogh argues, "in refusing to comply [with your wishes, no one] fails to recognize that your life belongs to you" (p. 170). The objection might be recast in the following way: it is impermissible paternalism to fail to *promote* the autonomy of an individual who wishes to die by physician-assisted death. But now the objection is rather weak. Autonomy is but one value among others; if those other relevant values (such as well-being, dignity, etc.) count strongly against assistance, one would have reasons of sufficient strength not to grant the individual's wish to die. As Den Hartogh argues:

> Nothing is... wrong if other people refuse to help... because they believe that such help would only be harmful. On the contrary, if [people] provide such 'help' out of indifference for the other person's fate, they are morally criticisable, at least for lack of concern (p. 170; see Foot 1977).

The appeal to care brings us to the status objection to paternalism, which we may treat briefly. I take it that Den Hartogh considers status, like dignity, to be a buck-passing value with a qualification dimension (p. 169). The qualification dimension of status requires respect for self-governance, but we have already seen that a refusal of assistance on grounds of harm is not disrespectful of autonomy. Further, the qualification dimension of status might also mandate an attitude of care or concern. As Den Hartogh argues:

> By refusing [assistance thought not to be in your interests], it seems to me, [an agent] only shows concern for you, not any lack of respect. He leaves you full responsibility for your own actions, and only takes an equal responsibility for his own (p. 171).

These points lead to the conclusion that the status objection to paternalism in the context of physician assisted fails.

Note that thus far, the examples used to discuss the self-governance and status objections have been dyadic: involving B's refusal to help A. But they apply also in the triadic, indirect paternalism case in which C stays B's hand: "if your autonomy isn't infringed upon by a person's refusal to help you [when assistance isn't in your interest], it cannot be infringed upon either by the state obligating that person to refuse" (p. 170). A maintains their self-governance or status, while B merely has additional C-given reasons not to promote A's autonomy.

In this section, I outlined Den Hartogh's Track 2 account of the permissibility of full-blown physician-assisted death. In my view, it lies on robust foundations. Criteria that supplement an autonomous wish to die may be required by the values of dignity and care or concern; and such criteria need not be impermissibly paternalistic. We may now move to the more evaluative part of the article, in which I consider the nature and justification of Den Hartogh's dual track model.

The nature and justification of the dual-track model: dual or single gauge?

On the railways, tracks have gauge — the transverse distance between the rails. While there is a 'standard' railway gauge (1435 mm), it is in fact one choice available among many. Sometimes, tracks of different gauge run to the same destination. Here, the system operator may build *dual* gauge tracks to accommodate different wheelset widths — often a track with three rails.

We might characterise Den Hartogh's dual-track model for access to lethal drugs and full-blown physician-assisted death as dual gauge. Track 1 has a pair of rails exemplifying the value of autonomy. Track 2 shares a rail in common with Track 1 and has one rail of its own, reflecting how self-determination in combination with other values justifies full-blown physician-assisted death.

In this section, I challenge the conception of the dual-track model as dual gauge. I argue that the nature of Tracks 1 and 2 is the same: deblocking access to lethal drugs is assistance to die. Further, I argue that it is better to justify Track 1 in the same way as Track 2: by appeal to self-determination and other goods.

Deblocking access to lethal drugs: non-assistance?
Recall that on Den Hartogh's Track 1, mere provision of lethal drugs to an autonomous person "is not really a form of assistance [to die], it is lifting a blockade" (p. 82). To wit, lethal medication may be prescribed on the basis of self-determination alone. I have doubts.

Den Hartogh develops his 'lifting a blockade' argument by reference to a baseline state of affairs:

> In a 'state of nature' people would have unlimited access. Then the state comes along, limiting access, for whatever reason. If the state then makes an exception for people who have chosen death without undue pressure and after ample consideration, it only stops interfering with their freedom. It stands out of the way (p. 82).

A difficulty with this strategy is that the causal dimension of conduct — here, whether something I do or allow restores you to a position you occupied before my intervention — is not conclusive of whether I assist you. My agential involvement and whether it amounts to assistance, aid, facilitation etc. depends in addition on facts about my state of mind: if I intend or foresee (to some relevant degree) that you will achieve your ends, the centrality of your ends to my plans, my thought and effort etc. (Wedgwood 2009, p. 334-335). In short, it is compatible with helping an individual out of a situation that one is the reason they are in it.

Say that I am a naval captain blockading a port. Now imagine that, in virtue of some behaviour of mine, the blockade lifts. It seems an open question whether I assist you. Suppose that I sympathise with your cause and — against the orders of superiors — I let your ships in or out. If found out, I am surely liable for treason, *viz*, assisting the enemy. This seems a clear case in which one both lifts a blockade and assists another to achieve their ends.

Let me bring this point home more precisely with regard to Track 1. An individual (P) has an interest in deciding the manner and moment of death (interest D). Interest D can be fulfilled (perhaps to differing degrees) by various means: D_1, D_2, etc. Say that D_1 is a refusal of life-prolonging treatment, D_2 is lethal medication. Suppose further (and plausibly) that a third party (T) controls D_2. T might be an individual, or the State (or both).

There seems to be a difference in strength of causal agential involvement between D_1 and D_2 that partly determines whether one assists you. In D_1 it seems difficult, other things equal,[6] to describe T's respect for P's refusal of life-prolonging treatment as assistance, since a refusal *excludes* others from exerting a causal influence that alters the underlying state of affairs. Of course, T's respect is part of the causal story of the outcomes attendant on P's refusal; my point is rather that T's causal involvement is too low when P dies by means of D_1. By contrast, in D_2, in making available lethal medication to P, T is a central feature of the causal explanation of how and when P dies. Where the means of death is D_2, the degree of T's causal involvement opens the question of assistance.

As I argue above, however, the causal dimension of agential involvement is not sufficient to determine whether T assists P to die. In addition, I suggest that P's ends must count among T's reasons for action. Certainly, this will be the case in D_2 if T shares with P the plan that P die by means of lethal medication. It may well be that something short of intention — such as T's knowledge and acceptance of P's ends — suffices too. We need not dwell on this potentially contentious detail of assistance in respect of Track 1. For here, it is plausible that when T grants P access to lethal means in full knowledge that P intends to use it for suicide, T intends the supply of lethal

---

6   I make the *ceteris paribus* qualification because things may be more complicated when the offer of palliative care accompanies refusal of treatment (and indeed stopping eating and drinking) (Den Hartogh chapters 7 and 8).

medication as a means to *P*'s ends.[7] It is the very point of regimes for lawful assisted death that one may openly intend to assist an individual to access otherwise unavailable lethal means in order to control the manner and moment of death.

At this juncture, it pays to consider an objection.[8] It might be said that, notwithstanding the argument above, individuals granted access to lethal drugs under Track 1 are not assisted by the third parties who assess or certify that the former meets the condition or status of being autonomous. Recalling that Den Hartogh envisages that physicians perform this task (p. 89), the objection holds that it is problematic to describe Track 1 cases as 'physician-assisted suicide'; to the extent that there is a suicide assistor, it is the party who *dispenses* the medication — for example, a pharmacist who acts on the physician's certification. One way to characterise the objection is that it goes to the *quality*, as opposed to degree, of *T*'s causal involvement in *P*'s death.

In circumstances of an integrated (and possibly hierarchical) division of labour, we do not typically carve up agency as if it were prosciutto in a deli slicer. Here, it is not only the person who performs a task on another's instructions or clearance — perhaps under some obligation — who is a participant in the relevant activity. The gatekeeper who orders '*raise!*' is implicated as much as (if not more than) the operator of the portcullis winch. Similarly, we might regard a physician who certifies and prescribes lethal drugs to an individual under Track 1 as much as (if not more) an assistor in suicide as a pharmacist under an obligation to dispense medication on presentation of a valid prescription. But perhaps this response does not address the gist of the objection. What if, against the usual run of things, physicians were only to certify an individual's autonomous status and pharmacists empowered to dispense on certification alone? Rather than unity and hierarchy, we might observe a degree of independence of function. We might describe physicians as *mere* gatekeepers, insofar as they declare, rather than mandate. Can such actors be assistors? At least sometimes, yes.

In many jurisdictions, there exists a system for mandatory periodic assessment of the roadworthiness of vehicles in the mode of the British MOT or the French *contrôle technique*. Examiners at test stations authorised by the State inspect vehicles for faults commensurate with the status 'unroadworthy',

---

7   Of course, I do not underestimate some people's capacity for self-deception such that they might credibly deblock access to lethal drugs for an individual they know to hold a wish to die and yet not intend the use of these drugs as a means to suicide.

8   I owe this concern to Gijs van Donselaar.

the absence of this condition being required, as a matter of law, to drive on publicly accessible roads. All being well, one's vehicle receives certification of roadworthiness. The task performed enables the motorist to evince that the vehicle in question has met the requisite criteria for presence on the roads. The roadworthiness examiner occupies the position of gatekeeper and service provider. In my view, it would not be misleading or an act of linguistic violence for an assessment centre to trade under the slogan *'Helping you to stay on the road!'*. Even when the operator offers only testing and none of the services of a repair garage. It is not a distortion to hold that vehicle test providers assist motorists. (Notwithstanding that the latter might begrudge the necessity of the former's aid.)

Third parties authorised to assess and certify the autonomous status of individuals who wish to access lethal drugs under Track 1 occupy a similar position to roadworthiness examiners. Track 1 assessors control access to lethal drugs and in performing their gatekeeping function, they provide a service to individuals who go on to die by these means (and indeed those who do not). It is not problematic, I argue, to describe the exercise of this office as assistance: what is done enables individuals to demonstrate their eligibility for an otherwise legally restricted activity. If Track 1 assistors are physicians and there is a unity of prescription and dispensation, this adds a further dimension to the assistance provided.

Thus the 'assessors are not assistors' objection fails. Note, however, that its articulation and response help also to clarify the position of the State when it permits activities such as motoring or assisted suicide on satisfaction of some eligibility criterion or criteria. If the State establishes an official process governing access to some restricted activity, it 'lifts a blockade' but does not merely 'stand out of the way'. Rather, its activity — assuming effectiveness of the institutional framework — facilitates individuals' enjoyment of their legal entitlements.

To summarise, I have argued that the mere supply of lethal medication is both 'lifting a blockade' and assisting suicide, at least within a Track 1 structure. It follows that the nature of Track 1 is the same as that of Track 2; both involve third party assistance to die. The difference between the tracks is the degree of assistance. And so the question arises whether self-determination alone is a tenable normative foundation for Track 1. If Den Hartogh's argument for the nature and justification of Track 2 — physician-assisted death as joint action — are any guide, possibly not. As we shall see, this need not, however, be fatal to Track 1.

Before we move on, there is a further issue with Den Hartogh's use of a state of nature baseline that I wish to raise. It strikes me as problematic to hold that one has a natural freedom to access lethal medication such as barbiturates — substances that are fruits of civil society. Admittedly, this worry is somewhat hostage to one's conception of the state of nature.[9] Since it is not strictly necessary to ventilate the concern, I shall forego developing the issue in the interests of economy of discussion.

Justifying deblocking access to legal drugs: beyond autonomy
Den Hartogh justifies mere access to lethal drugs by appeal to the value of autonomy or self-determination alone. This normative footing relies on a conceptual argument whose merits I challenged in the previous section. If supply of lethal medication for the purposes of suicide is assistance to die, it seems less tenable that one has a right of access to such drugs on the normative basis of self-determination alone. As we saw in the exposition of Den Hartogh's Track 2 argument, the greater the degree of agential involvement, the greater the assistor's answerability for helping another to die; and the lesser weight an answer justifying assistance merely in terms of the autonomy of the individual who dies.

I should clarify, however, that I am not against a right of mere access to lethal medication for suicide. My project is to offer a normative basis for the right different to Den Hartogh's argument for Track 1, but along the lines of his account of Track 2.

It is important to distinguish the conditions for the enjoyment or exercise of a right and its justification. I may have some right to choose freely — that is, merely in virtue of being an autonomous agent — but having a right to choose freely need not entail that the value of choosing is the (sole) reason I may choose. Yet Den Hartogh seems to reject this view of the justification of rights of autonomous free choice in his account of Track 1. Consider the analogy he draws between 'lifting the blockade' on lethal medication and access to guns:

> if the state allows access [to guns] in some cases, for example for shooting sports or hunting, it does not facilitate these activities, it only abstains from hindering or thwarting them. The default is unlimited access; access is only limited for some acknowledged reasons, to the extent that these reasons require. If they don't apply, access is free again (p. 92).

Den Hartogh's argument seems to be that our rights of autonomous free choice consist in the residue of our autonomy. We have the right to choose

9   Thank you to Gijs van Donselaar for urging caution here.

freely just when we are autonomous and autonomy has greatest weight after specification in light of other values and considerations. However, this is merely a contingent truth.

Let us grant that one has a natural freedom to access guns. Further, let me concede that in the state of nature it is the value of autonomy that explains why one has a right to access guns. I would challenge the view, however, that in a state of civil society the allocation of freedoms is justified by the overriding reason that applies in the state of nature. It is not obvious that appeal to one's natural freedom is sufficient to justify rights of autonomous free choice when natural freedom is no longer in play. Should some matter lie within an individual's area of private sovereignty, this may be in virtue of *plural positive* justifications.

Regarding Den Hartogh's guns example, we might hold that access is granted in contemporary circumstances not only because of the value of self-determination, but rather also for other reasons. We might allow shooting sports because there is a value of play (or recreation). We might also allow hunting because of the value of tradition. (Perhaps also or alternatively — depending on the quarry — because of the value of some ecosystem.) Our private domain rights may be a function not only of autonomy and its counterweights; instead a cluster or composite of interests on both sides of the scale.

To return to the right of mere access to lethal drugs under Track 1, it is plausible that the right has this more complex structure. That is, values other than self-determination determine whether the satisfaction of interest D by this means falls within the scope of an individual's rights of autonomous free choice.

Consider the following "'bad' means" example. An individual autonomously requests mere access to restricted medication that, rather than bringing about an easeful death, guarantees a passing that is nasty, brutish, and long. (No doubt there are manifold possibilities.) I imagine that we would struggle to grant such a request or concede that the individual in question has a right of access to such means of death. Our reasons would align with Den Hartogh's "basic moral considerations" (p. 31), and those advanced in the account of Track 2 (pp. 163-174): suicide by such 'bad' means constitutes self-abasement, is so imprudent it exceeds the margin of content-independence etc. It would be impermissible to assist a suicide of this nature.

The 'bad' means example is revealing of the actual normative grounding of Track 1. We might grant individuals a right of mere access to lethal medication not only because they autonomously wish to control the manner and moment of death, but also because assisting individuals to die in this way exemplifies other important values. On the basis of the preceding discussion, these would include well-being (pp. 167-174), as well as dignity (p. 74). Den Hartogh might add solidarity and relationships (p. 74).[10]

If my argument is persuasive, the normative justification of Den Hartogh's Track 1 is both structurally and substantively similar to that of Track 2. Autonomy is an individually necessary condition for the permissibility of granting a right of mere access to lethal drugs, but sufficient only when combined with other individually necessary conditions.

Before we conclude, I should address a question that may linger. If the normative justification of Tracks 1 and 2 is similar, why permit mere access to lethal drugs on the basis of autonomy alone? The answer, I submit, lies in the reduced degree of agential involvement of Track 1 assistors compared to those of Track 2, and the effect their involvement has on the permissibility of their conduct (Black 2021). In virtue of the higher degree of agential involvement in Track 2 cases, assistors must be more attentive to the goodness of the state of affairs they jointly bring about with the individual who dies. In Track 1 cases, assistors are less agentially involved and the means prescribed are expected to be safe (at least relative to other means of suicide). Track 1 assistors may take some comfort that their agency is implicated in realising a minimally, comparatively good (albeit not necessarily best) state of affairs. I suggest that this explanation plausibly aligns with the reasons we might hold for allowing mere access to lethal drugs for hard classes.

Conclusion

I have offered a critical reading of Govert den Hartogh's 'dual-track' model for assisted death, focusing on the argument Den Hartogh offers for Track 1: mere access to lethal drugs on the basis of an autonomous request. I have argued, *pace* Den Hartogh, that permitting mere access to lethal medication may be both 'lifting a blockade' and assisting an individual to die. This conclusion about the *nature* of Track 1 opens the question of the sufficiency of autonomy as its sole normative basis. A revised account of the *justification* for Track 1 is possible, however. I argued that Track 1 assistance may be permissible on the same grounds as Den Hartogh provides for Track 2 (full-blown physician assisted death), *viz*, autonomy in conjunction with other values, including dignity and well-being (albeit in a different mix). In

---

10   Den Hartogh makes the case for family assistance in suicide as an extension of the individual's Track 1 rights. I have omitted discussion of this interesting material for reasons of space.

this sense, rather than conceive of Den Hartogh's model for assisted death as 'dual-track', dual gauge, we might rather consider mere access to lethal drugs and full-blown physician assisted death as two services on a single normative gauge.

I suggest that my single gauge model of mere access to lethal drugs and full-blown physician-assisted death is philosophically more plausible and pragmatically advantageous compared to Den Hartogh's dual gauge account. The single gauge model owns up to mere prescription of lethal medication as assistance to die, and thereby avoids the potential charge of attempting to solve a difficult normative issue by conceptual means. Moreover, in making a right of mere access to lethal medication depend on more than autonomy for its justification, we broaden its normative basis from respect for what individuals autonomously will to what we might owe them as a matter of respect and concern; this may broaden its political appeal. Though perhaps we must concede that permitting mere access to lethal drugs instantiates the values of respect and concern in only a qualified and comparative way. Maybe that is enough.

About the author

Dr. Isra Black (isra.black@ucl.ac.uk) is a Lecturer in Health Law and Research Impact and Engagement Lead in the Faculty of Laws, University College London.

Literature

Atkins, K., "Autonomy and the Subjective Character of Experience," *Journal of Applied Philosophy* 17 (2000) 1, 71-79.
Black, I., "Refusing Life-Prolonging Medical Treatment and the ECHR," *Oxford Journal of Legal Studies* 38 (2018) 2, 299-327.
Black, I., "A Pro Tanto Moral Case for Assisted Death" in Westwood, S. (Ed.), *Regulating the end of life: death rights*. London: Routledge 2021.
Dworkin, G., *The Theory and Practice of Autonomy*. Cambridge: Cambridge University Press, 1988.
Feinberg, J., *Harm to Self*. New York: Oxford University Press 1986.
Foot, P., "Euthanasia," *Philosophy & Public Affairs* 6 (1977) 2, 85-112.
Den Hartogh, G., *What Kind of Death. The Ethics of Determining One's Own Death*. New York: Routledge, 2023.

Hurka, T., "Why Value Autonomy?," *Social Theory and Practice* 13 (1987) 3, 361-382.

Kamm, F.M., "Physician-Assisted Suicide, the Doctrine of Double Effect, and the Ground of Value," *Ethics* 109 (1999) 3, 586-605.

Mackenzie, C., "Relational Autonomy, Normative Authority and Perfectionism," *Journal of Social Philosophy* 39 (2008) 4, 512-533.

Nagel, T., "Personal Rights and Public Space," *Philosophy & Public Affairs* 24 (1995) 2, 83-107.

Raz, J., *The Morality of Freedom*. Oxford: Clarendon Press, 1986.

Raz, J., "Death in Our Life," *Journal of Applied Philosophy* 30 (2013) 1, 1-11.

Richardson, H.S., "Specifying Norms as a Way to Resolve Concrete Ethical Problems," *Philosophy and Public Affairs* 19 (1990) 4, 279-310.

Sumner, L., *Assisted Death: A Study in Ethics andLlaw*. Oxford: Oxford University Press, 2011.

Wedgwood, R., "Intrinsic Values and Reasons for Action," *Philosophical Issues* 19 (2009), 321-342.

The Changing (and Multifaceted) Role of the Principle of Self-Determination in the Dutch Euthanasia Practice

Esther Pans[1]

Abstract
This contribution deals with the role of the principle of self-determination in the current Dutch euthanasia practice. The focus lies on the concrete elaborations of the principle of self-determination in law and practice. I distinguish between self-determination as a dynamic, diffuse and risky principle. I analyze these three characteristics in the light of the current developments in the Dutch euthanasia practice. My conclusion is that the attempts to broaden the influence of the principle of self-determination within the law is – to a certain extent – rather successful and can be justified by the societal developments and the nature of the Dutch Euthanasia Act. The principle of self-determination is reflected in almost all elements of the law and it is in the spirit of the law to allow more room for self-determination if societal developments give rise to this and if this is possible in a safe way. Attempts to allow more room for self-determination outside the law have not been successful and involve too many risks for society.

Keywords: law review, moral justification of euthanasia, the right to self-determination, Dutch Act on Euthanasia and Physician-Assisted Suicide, the right to die.

---

1   This article has been published in *Tijdschrift voor Gezondheidsrecht* 2023/6 in Dutch in a slightly modified version. The author thanks Jurriaan de Haan and Henri Wijsbek for discussion.

Gijs van Donselaar, Peter Rijpkema, and Henri Wijsbek (eds), *The Ethics of Determining One's Own Death. Essays on Den Hartogh's What Kind of Death.*
Taylor & Francis Group, 2025
DOI: https://doi.org/10.5117/FEP2024.1.006.PANS

Introduction

It is and remains a fascinating question: what is the role of the principle of self-determination in the Dutch euthanasia[2] practice? What is the weight of this principle in the ethical force field surrounding euthanasia? Has the principle of self-determination become increasingly important in recent years and has it finally – after all – become the supporting force behind the Dutch euthanasia policy? In recent years, there does seem to be a renewed emphasis on self-determination, as the latest law review signals.[3] Developments in that direction can be found within interpretations of the law. These developments seem to indicate that patients' influence in the euthanasia process is increasing. This is visible in the assessment review of euthanasia cases by the Regional Review Committees. There are also developments outside the law, which are not so successful in legal terms, but which do show that there is a call from society for more self-determination in end-of-life issues.[4]

Expressions of self-determination

Let us take a closer look at the principle of self-determination. My aim is to approach the principle as concretely as possible. Self-determination is an abstract principle, but it has many concrete elaborations within the context of euthanasia. So, in order to get a better grip and more insight into the principle of self-determination, I focus my attention on its concrete elaborations in law and practice. There are three characteristics of the principle of self-determination.

Self-determination as a dynamic concept
Indeed, a stronger call for self-determination can be heard in the Netherlands in recent years, but (at the same time) contrary movements can also be seen. The picture is ambiguous. In terms of numbers, one can observe that euthanasia is becoming more 'popular': it is more common. Since the law

---

2 In this article "euthanasia" stands for "euthanasia and physician-assisted suicide".
3 A. van der Heide et al., *Vierde evaluatie Wet toetsing levensbeëindiging op verzoek en hulp bij zelfdoding*, Den Haag: ZonMw 2023. p. 299-301.
4 See for an overview of (Dutch) news messages on euthanasia: https://www.nvve.nl. See for an ethical approach: G.A. den Hartogh, *What kind of death. The ethics of determining one's own death*, Routledge 2023. See for a description of the societal developments in recent years: H. Weyers, *Euthanasie in Nederland 2002-2022*, Den Haag: Boom Juridisch 2022.

came into force there has been a steady increase in the share of euthanasia in the total number of deaths.[5] To be precise: while in 2015 it was 4,5%, in 2021 it was 5,3%. Furthermore, over the years euthanasia has increased shortening of life span. In other words: euthanasia is increasingly performed at a stage in which patients still have a considerable life expectancy. In 2015, 15% of the cases involved life shortening of more than 6 months, in 2021 this was 19%. It is not only in the practice of reported euthanasia cases that one can see a heavier weight of the patient's voice, but also in the assessment review of the cases by the Regional Review Committees. In the latest review of the law, published in May 2023, the researchers conclude that there is a tendency to place more emphasis on patient autonomy than before. According to the researchers this is manifested in the following developments[6]:
– More emphasis on the personal experience of suffering;
– Less emphasis on (the review of) treatment alternatives;
– More (room for interpretation of) weight for living wills.

On the other hand, the law review also shows that the Dutch are very much attached to the doctor's role in euthanasia.[7] The study review shows that there (still) is a lot of support in society for the doctor's central position. So, while it is true that Dutch citizens also value autonomy, they do not want to get rid of the doctor's involvement. Another quite surprising finding is that the proportion of people who think that family members should also be allowed to provide assistance in suicide has decreased significantly. While in 2016 this was 46%, in 2022 this was 26%. This drop is all the more striking because of the media coverage of the Cooperation Last Will and the draft bill on 'Completed Life' of the (liberal) political party D66 during this period[8] (although these initiatives are related to dying via the "autonomous route", so there is no role for doctors nor for family members). In short, if we zoom in on the various concrete actual societal developments of self-determination, a highly mixed and contradictory picture emerges. There are developments in favour of more self-determination (towards moderate or more far-going forms of self-determination), and also developments in the other direction.

---

5   A. van der Heide et al. 2023, p. 288, 294-295 en 307.
6   A. van der Heide et al. 2023, pp. 299-302.
7   A. van der Heide et al. 2023, p. 253-256 and 293.
8   Wet toetsing levenseindebegeleiding van ouderen op verzoek (Wtlo), Kamerstukken 2019/2020, *35534*.

Self-determination as a diffuse concept

What groups do we have in mind when we speak of more room for self-determination in end-of-life issues? Do we have particular groups of citizens with certain characteristics in mind? For a long time, in politics and elsewhere, there was this image of elderly people, mainly very old, who at some point had become "weary of life", tired of living. This concept was often referred to as a "balanced suicide". But was this assumption right? In other words: how homogeneous is the group of elderly people with a death wish who are not seriously ill? In 2020 a much-discussed report by Van Wijngaarden and others was published on this topic: the Perspective Study.[9] There was much to do about whether the estimate of the group of non-seriously ill elderly people with a death wish is correct. It is said to be only close to 1% (0.95%) of the Dutch people over 55 years old. I will not get into that discussion here. However, I do find it interesting to take a closer look at the characteristics of the studied group.

The Perspective Study revealed that the group of elderly people who want to die and is not seriously ill, is mixed and vulnerable. Besides that, it also showed that their death wishes appear to be changeable. The circumstances of their daily lives affect their death wishes. The study shows that a death wish can diminish or disappear over the years, even in old age. A large majority of the subjects is found to have physical and mental symptoms. It is certainly not a "healthy" group. Furthermore, the group turns out to be less elderly than expected. More than 75% were younger than 75 years. Among people with an active death wish there is an overrepresentation of women (67%), people of a low level of education (44%) and people of a lower social-economic class (53%). Summarized, the group is more problematic in terms of vulnerability and more mixed than previously expected and their death wishes are more changeable than expected. On the basis of this Study it seems to be controversial to argue in favor of more room for self-determination in end-of-life issues for elderly people with a death wish who are not seriously ill.

Self-determination as a risky concept

The absolute opposite of self-determination is being killed against one's own will. Anyone who, inspired by the principle of self-determination, drafts legal regulations for access to lethal drugs, but fails to regulate properly how

---

9   E. van Wijngaarden et al., *Perspectieven op ouderen met een doodswens zonder dat zij ernstig ziek zijn: de mensen en de cijfers*, Den Haag: ZonMw 2020.

to prevent abuse, creates a life-threatening law. Given the stakes, the risk of abuse is real. That's why all the draft bills that aim to regulate this topic fall on the drawing board.[10] Essentially, in my opinion the critics always comes down to the following objections[11]:
- No (adequate) way to test whether the person really wants to die (internal aspect of voluntariness of the request);
- No (adequate) way to test on whether there is third-party pressure (the external aspect of the voluntariness of the request);
- No (adequate) way to test on whether all is done to improve the circumstances that may determine the death wish;
- Potential problems with the distribution of lethal drugs: no safeguards to prevent third parties to get access to the drugs, intentionally or unintentionally;
- Potential problems concerning the medical complications that can occur after taking the drugs.

Concluding remarks

So, what can we conclude? One can distinguish between attempts to broaden the influence of the principle of self-determination within the law and outside the law. On that, I can be clear: that is not a fruitful idea. Let us cherish what we have. Let us embrace the Dutch Euthanasia Law. The law is a careful construction. The principle of self-determination is reflected in almost all elements of the law. Furthermore, it is also fully in the spirit of the Dutch Euthanasia Act to allow more room for self-determination if societal developments give rise to this and if this is possible in a safe way and within the legal framework. And this is precisely the flexibility the legislator intended (to offer) by opting for so called 'open norms' in the law. In my opinion the law does justice to the interests of doctors, patients and the society at large. Within the law, a balance has been achieved between the principles of self-determination, mercy and the sanctity of life. This balance is not static. The weight these three principles carry in the practice and assessment of euthanasia may change. If society is ready for it, if the call from society for more emphasis on self-determination is strong and straightforward, much can be done within the law. And much is already happening right now. In short, within the law there is indeed a development of more

---

10   https://www.raadvanstate.nl/adviezen/@121919/w13-20-0284-iii/
11   E. Pans, "Op de pil van Drion kun je lang wachten", *De Volkskrant* 1 november 2016.

room for self-determination. I welcome that development. But outside the law I do not see any realistic possibilities. The protective mechanisms of the Dutch Euthanasia Act are indispensable.

About the author

Esther Pans (e.pans@expertisecentrumeuthanasie.nl) works as a Legal Counsel of *Expertisecentrum Euthanasie* in The Hague and as a Senior Researcher at the Faculty of Law of the *Vrije Universiteit* in Amsterdam, The Netherlands.

Like a Peat Fire. The Impact of the Right to Self-Determination on the (Dutch) Law on Euthanasia

Jurriaan de Haan[1]

Abstract

This contribution deals with the moral justification of euthanasia. Initially, in the process towards legalizing euthanasia in the Netherlands the right to self-determination was the driving force. However, it is widely accepted that Dutch law on euthanasia that was passed in 2001 is based on mercy. In this respect, the early work of Den Hartogh has been influential. So, the principle of respect for autonomy and the principle of beneficence both seem to play a role in justifying euthanasia. Why exactly do we need those two principles, and what exactly are their complimentary roles? These are important questions that Den Hartogh has put on the agenda. In recent years several initiatives have been undertaken to increase the possibilities for euthanasia and assisted suicide. Again, these initiatives are driven by the right to self-determination. In this contribution the focus will be on this development regarding the underlying principles, with attention for the question how Den Hartogh's dual track theory should be placed in this development.

Keywords: moral justification of euthanasia, the right to self-determination, principle of beneficence or mercy, Den Hartogh's dual track theory.

---

1 The author works as a judge in the Netherlands. This contribution reflects only the author's views. He thanks Govert den Hartogh and Esther Pans for discussion. This contribution is the text of his talk at the conference the Ethics of End-of-Life Decisions. It has been edited for publication in this journal. The author has benefited from the editorial comments by Henri Wijsbek.

Gijs van Donselaar, Peter Rijpkema, and Henri Wijsbek (eds), *The Ethics of Determining One's Own Death. Essays on Den Hartogh's What Kind of Death.*
Taylor & Francis Group, 2025
DOI: https://doi.org/10.5117/FEP2024.1.007.HAAN

Introduction

This contribution deals with the moral justification of euthanasia. This is one of the important topics in Den Hartogh's book *What kind of death. The ethics of determining one's own death*.[2] Is euthanasia a matter of respect for autonomy or of mercy? The right to self-determination and the principle of beneficence both seem to play a role in justifying euthanasia. Why exactly do we need those two principles, and what exactly are their complimentary roles? These are important questions that Den Hartogh has put on the agenda. As we will see, Den Hartogh's early work has been influential in the debate. In his book he has added to this an in-depth analysis of his dual track theory of euthanasia and assisted suicide.

In this contribution I will put the debate about the underlying principles in a historical perspective. First we will see that in the process towards legalizing euthanasia in the Netherlands the right to self-determination initially was the driving force. Subsequently it has gained acceptance that Dutch law on euthanasia is based on mercy. In recent years several initiatives have been undertaken to increase the possibilities for euthanasia and assisted suicide. Again, these initiatives are driven by the right to self-determination.

Den Hartogh's alternative to the dominant view

Proponents of the legalization of euthanasia often appeal to the right to self-determination. Beside the right to self-determination, the principle of beneficence or mercy plays an important role in the debate. Den Hartogh writes in his book: "But it has rarely been discussed why exactly we need those two principles, and what exactly are their complimentary roles".[3]

Does he not thereby sell himself short? Already in 1996 he addressed this issue in his article in the Dutch journal *Recht en Kritiek*.[4] In that article he pointed out that there was a dominant view on the justification of euthanasia. This view entails that the right to self-determination includes the right of a person to end his own life if he himself believes that it has lost its value

---

2   G.A. den Hartogh, *What kind of death. The ethics of determining one's own death*, Routledge 2023, especially ch. 9.
3   Den Hartogh 2023, p. 8.
4   G.A. den Hartogh, "Recht op de dood? Zelfbeschikking en barmhartigheid als rechtvaardigingsgronden voor euthanasie", *Recht en Kritiek* 1996, 148-169.

as well as that he can then authorize others to help him do so. This was the view of the health care lawyer Leenen[5] and the patient organization the Dutch Association for Voluntary Euthanasia (NVVE).

In *Recht en Kritiek* Den Hartogh has developed an alternative to the dominant view. His view was (and still is) that not the right to self-determination but the principle of beneficence or mercy is the ultimate moral justification for euthanasia.

Den Hartogh claimed that his alternative view – that euthanasia is a matter of mercy – provides a more coherent interpretation not only of our moral intuitions but also of the case law in the Netherlands at the time. This is because the Supreme Court of the Netherlands had accepted the defence of necessity for doctors who had performed euthanasia upon the request of a patient, in the sense that a doctor may have faced a conflict of duties: on the one hand, the duty to preserve life and on the other hand, the duty to relieve his patient's suffering.[6] Den Hartogh noted that the latter duty does not appeal to the patient's right to self-determination but to the principle of beneficence.

Legalizing euthanasia

In 2001 the law on euthanasia was passed in the Netherlands, making it the first country to legalize euthanasia.[7] This law can be regarded as a codification of the case law at the time. As such it was the (provisional) result of a social process, and above all its formal recognition.[8] In particular, the law codifies the so-called 'due care criteria'. The two most important being: first that doctor must be convinced that the request for euthanasia is voluntary and well-considered and second that the doctor must be convinced that the patient's suffering is unbearable with no prospect of improvement.

After euthanasia was legalized in the Netherlands, it was also legalized in other countries. Soon Belgium followed, and more recently Spain, Canada,

---

5 See H.J.J. Leenen, *Handboek Gezondheidsrecht Deel 1: Rechten van mensen in de gezondheidszorg*, Alphen a/d Rijn: Samson H.D. Tjeenk Willink 1994, chapter 11.
6 HR 27 November 1984, *NJ* 1985, 106 (*Schoonheim*) and HR 21 June 1994, *NJ* 1994, 656 (*Chabot*).
7 See the text of the law, as well as the short introduction to it in my article in the *Medical Law Review*: J.P. de Haan, "The New Dutch Law on Euthanasia", *Medical Law Review* 10 (2002) 1, 57-75.
8 J.P. de Haan, "De symbolische betekenis van de nieuwe euthanasiewet", *Ars Aequi* 50 (2001) 11, 882-884.

New Zealand and Australia.[9] All these countries also have requirements regarding the patient's request and his condition. So both the expression of the will and the patient's best interests matter.

This again raises the question concerning the underlying medical-ethical principle. The question that Den Hartogh answered back in 1996 for the Dutch situation. Is this the principle of respect for autonomy or the principle of beneficence or both?[10]

Mercy as the justification of the legalization of euthanasia

In her PhD-thesis, Pans has thoroughly analyzed all parliamentary documents on the law on euthanasia. She found that the government indicates that relief of suffering is the fundamental reason for creating the possibility of euthanasia. On the basis of her analyses, she concludes that the principle of mercy seems to be the main justification for the Dutch law on euthanasia.[11] In any case, the government emphatically denied that the law is (covertly) based on the right to self-determination.

It has gained acceptance in the Netherlands that mercy is the justification for euthanasia, and that the patient's request – as a expression of self-determination – is (only) a necessary condition. Authors who observe this always refer to the work of Den Hartogh.[12] Using the terminology from my 2002 article in *Bioethics*[13], he now characterizes the relationship in his book as follows: "The interest of the patient is a contributing factor to the justification of euthanasia, his consent only an enabling factor".[14]

---

9   See Den Hartogh 2023, p. 2n1. See for a comparison of the laws in these countries the latest evaluation report of the Dutch law on euthanasia, A. van der Heide et al., *Vierde evaluatie Wet toetsing levensbeëindiging op verzoek en hulp bij zelfdoding*, Den Haag: ZonMw 2023 pp. 77-86.
10 For an account of these medical-ethical principles I refer to the standard work by T.L. Beauchamp en J.F. Childress, *Principles of Medical Ethics* (New York: Oxford University Press).
11 E. Pans, *De normatieve grondslagen van het Nederlandse euthanasierecht*, Nijmegen: Wolf Legal Publishers 2006, p. 144.
12 See for example H. Weyers, *Euthanasie in Nederland 2002-2022*, Den Haag: Boomjuridisch 2022, p. 22. See also A. van der Heide et al. 2023, p. 247.
13 J. de Haan, "The Ethics of Euthanasia: Advocates' Perspectives", *Bioethics* 16 (2002) 2, 154-172 on p. 165. There I explain the distinction between contributing and enabling factors as follows. Contributing factors (or contributors) are features of a situation that contribute to the rightness (or wrongness) of an action. They play a right-making role, so to speak. Enabling factors (or enablers), on the other hand, are features that enable the right-making features to play their role, without playing that role themselves. Enablers switch contributors on, as it were.
14 Den Hartogh 2023, p. 180.

We can conclude that the dominant view of in particular Leenen has been replaced by the Den Hartogh's alternative. He has thus been influential (in the Dutch speaking world) when it comes to the view on the moral justification of euthanasia.

Social context

At the same time, it is clear that the law on euthanasia has come about in a social context in which individual autonomy is of increasing importance. The historical background in the Netherlands is an emancipation movement that started in the 1960s. There was a desire for freedom that manifested itself in many areas.[15]

This movement also reached health law, resulting for example in a legal basis for the right of patients to refuse medical treatment.[16] People wanted and still want control over their lives, including over the manner and time of their own death.

This interpretation of the right to self-determination is currently also legally recognized. It derives from article 8 of the European Convention of Human Rights, according to recent case law of the European Court of Human Rights.[17]

Furthermore, it is noticeable that people's desire to have a grip on when and how their life ends has not been satisfied by the Dutch law on euthanasia. There is a lot of support for this law, it is seen as an achievement,[18] but there seems to be a substantial group of people who want more.

Towards more self-determination

Due to the widespread idea that mercy is the justification for euthanasia, the right to self-determination had been buried, as it were. But like a peat fire, the need for individual autonomy has spread under the surface. And

---

15 See C.W. Maris, *Tolerance: Experiments with Freedom in the Netherlands*, Dordrecht: Springer, 2018.
16 Wet op de geneeskundige behandelingsovereenkomst (WGBO).
17 Notably ECHR 20 January 2011, 31322/07 (*Haas/Zwitserland*). For an overview of the legal developments to date R. Lawson, "Keuzevrijheid ten aanzien van het eigen levenseinde: Straatsburgse perspectieven", *NTM/NJCM-bull.* 2023/12.
18 See A. van der Heide et al 2023, chapter 7. It is also worth mentioning that the frequency of euthanasia continues to rise. This is reflected upon in the evaluation report on p. 294 and 295.

now, 20 years after the law came into force, it appears to be reemerging in various ways.

In this regard, I distinguish between pressure towards more self-determination within the framework of the law and outside the law (which is not to say that the initiatives to change the current law on euthanasia and introduce alternative regulations are always illegal).

Within the framework of the law

From the most recent evaluation report on the Dutch law on euthanasia, it can be gathered that more room for self-determination has been created within the framework of the law. In particular the due care criterion that there has to be unbearable suffering with no prospect of improvement has been given a more subjective interpretation. Greater importance is given to the input and the perception of the patient.[19] This is also reflected in the *Euthanasia Code*, the code used by the regional review committees to assess whether a case of euthanasia was in accordance with the requirements of careful practice.[20]

In addition, it is reported that advance directives have gained more significance.[21] It has become part of Dutch euthanasia practice (that the doctor may rely on an advance directive was part of the law from the outset) that doctors can perform euthanasia on the basis of an advance directive, for example – in exceptional cases and small numbers – in the case of patients in an advanced phase of dementia. This too contributes to the patients' autonomy.

Outside the law

Several initiatives have been undertaken to increase the legal possibilities for euthanasia and assisted suicide.

To begin with, there is an attempt in Dutch parliament to pass a new law to allow people who 'consider their lives completed' – but who do not suffer unbearably with no prospect of improvement as stated in the current law on euthanasia, in particular not because there is no disease present[22] – to end their lives.[23] According to this proposal, people who consider their lives

---

19   A. van der Heide et al. 2023, p. 272.
20   Euthanasia Code 2022, publication of the regional review committee, www.euthanasiecommissie.nl/euthanasiecode-2022, on p. 26 and p. 28.
21   A. van der Heide et al. 2023, p. 272.
22   This limitation of the scope of the law stems from case law, namely the *Brongersma*-ruling (HR 24 December 2002, NJ 2003/167).
23   Wet toetsing levenseindebegeleiding van ouderen op verzoek (Wtlo), Kamerstukken 2019/2020 35534 2.

completed should be able to do so with the help of a so-called end-of-life facilitator (not a doctor). Also there is an age limit; it is for people aged 75 and over. According to the explanatory memorandum, this bill is fundamentally based on the right to self-determination.[24] This bill was heavily criticized. An amended bill has since been introduced.[25]

Worth mentioning here are also the initiatives of the Cooperative Last Will (Coöperatie Laatste Wil).[26] These include a court case at the court in The Hague, with the aim that certain criminal provisions on euthanasia and assisted suicide will no longer be enforced. The argument was based on the right to self-determination as derived from the European Convention of Human Rights. The District Court of The Hague rejected the claim of Cooperative Last Will.[27] An appeal has been filed.

Beside this, according to reports in the press[28], members of the Cooperative Last Will have been active in providing information and drugs for self-euthanasia. This has led to criminal investigation, prosecution and conviction.[29]

Also the Dutch Association for Voluntary Euthanasia (NVVE) is still promoting more freedom of choice as far as end-of-life decisions are concerned, according to its website.[30]

Last but not least, in the meantime Den Hartogh has developed his dual track theory.[31] This theory entails that in addition to the current law – this is the first track – there should be a possibility for assisted suicide involving a doctor providing lethal means to a person – the second track. When applying the procedure of the law on euthanasia, the requirement of unbearable suffering with no prospect of improvement remains. Under the second track, there is an assessment of the doctor, but he only assesses the request, in particular whether the person involved is competent.

Interestingly, this second track is based on the right to self-determination. There has thus been a shift in Den Hartogh's thinking. Whereas in the 1990s he considered euthanasia and assisted suicide to be a matter of mercy (and he downplayed the principle of respect for autonomy), with his second track

---

24 Kamerstukken 2019/2020 35534 3.
25 https://d66.nl/nieuws/d66-dient-aangepaste-wet-voltooid-leven-in-bij-tweede-kamer/.
26 On the Cooperative Last Will see for example Weyers 2022, p. 274-278. See also the website of the Cooperative Last Will itself (laatstewil.nu).
27 Rechtbank Den Haag, 14 December 2022, ECLI:NL:RBDHA:2022:13394.
28 nos.nl/artikel/2483234-3-5-jaar-cel-voor-man-die-middel-x-voor-zelfdoding-leverde.
29 Rechtbank Oost-Brabant, 18 July 2023, ECLI:NL:RBOBR 2023:3640.
30 See www.nvve.nl.
31 Den Hartogh 2023, ch. 5.

he now finds himself in the camp of the more extreme proponents of the right to assisted suicide.[32]

The Pure Autonomy View vs the Joint View again

From the outset, I myself took a liberal, non-paternalistic view on the moral justification of euthanasia and assisted suicide. One of the propositions of my PhD-thesis was: euthanasia is a matter of respect for autonomy. In this way I argued against my supervisor Den Hartogh, who after all held that euthanasia is a matter of mercy.

So I was a supporter of the dominant view of Leenen and I elaborated on this view in my thesis from 2000.[33] The principle of respect for autonomy is the sole justifying principle. The patient's condition is relevant, but not because of mercy or the principle of beneficence. That condition is relevant because performing euthanasia on people who are not suffering unbearably with no prospect of improvement may be contrary to the public interest. The public interest is a broad concept. It can include the notion that life itself is valuable and worthy of protection. Further, it encompasses considerations of what we deem socially unacceptable consequences (for example the so-called slippery slope). Within the scope of this contribution, I can not elaborate on these considerations here.[34]

I later called this view – in my article in *Bioethics*[35] – the Pure Autonomy View. I referred to the alternatives, where euthanasia is justified by a combination of the principle of respect for autonomy and the principle of beneficence, as (different versions) of the Joint View.

Let me clarify the point of the Pure Autonomy View, using the developments in the past two decades. All countries that have legalized euthanasia have requirements regarding the patient's request and his condition. So both the expression of the will and the patient's best interests matter. It thus seems that the principle of respect for autonomy and the principle of beneficence both play a role in justifying euthanasia. My point is that this is a non sequitur. It is not necessarily the case that the principle

---

32 In the latest evaluation report of the Dutch law on euthanasia, five future scenarios are outlined – from leaving the law on euthanasia as it is to creating more possibilities for assisted suicide, including by non-physicians. See A. van der Heide et al. 2023, p. 279-284.

33 J. de Haan, *The Possibility of Moral Dilemmas*, diss. Universiteit van Amsterdam 2000, ch. 10.

34 See my PhD-thesis on p. 205 and my article in *Bioethics*, p. 166-167.

35 J. de Haan, "The Ethics of Euthanasia: Advocates' Perspectives", *Bioethics* 16 (2002) 2, 154-172.

of respect for autonomy and the principle of beneficence both play a justifying role. Conceptually there is room for a view in which the patient's condition is relevant, but not because of the principle of beneficence. There is a different explanation of why his condition is relevant, as I have pointed out above (the considerations concerning the public interest). My view is and was, not only that there is conceptual space for this, but that actually these principles do not both play a role in the moral justification of euthanasia and the principle of respect for autonomy is the sole justifying principle.

To come back to the questions put on the agenda by Den Hartogh that I mentioned before – 'Why exactly do we need those two principles, and what exactly are their complimentary roles?' – my reply is: we do not need the principle of beneficence or mercy, as justifying principle beside the principle of respect for autonomy. That we need it, is just an assumption, and I believe it is a false assumption. Also, in the Dutch context this principle doesn't fit in. This is because euthanasia is not considered to be normal medical practice by the legislator and the medical exception is not accepted by the courts.[36]

Public discussion

Looking back, I note that the Pure Autonomy View has been rejected in favor of the Joint View. Nowadays the idea of individual autonomy is rearing its head again. However, the discussion seems to be stuck. There is little prospect that the law on euthanasia will be reformed soon. Are we seeing the law of the handicap of a head start (wet van de remmende voorsprong)[37] here? Will the Netherlands, while being the first country in the world to legalize euthanasia, eventually end up with an outdated regulation?

How to make progress? The answer, in my view, should be: (more) public discussion. In particular, (more) discussion on the content and scope of the principle of respect for autonomy.

How far do we want to go with the right to self-determination? In any case, I believe that there are outer limits to take into account. First: the boundaries of the current law on euthanasia, so no criminal acts? Second: to apply safeguards and conditions, so as to protect the vulnerable and to

---

36 Pans 2006, p. 145-146 and 198.
37 The phenomenon is described by the Dutch historian Jan Romeijn in 1937 (nl.wikipedia.org/wiki/Wet_van_de_remmende_voorsprong; in English: en.wikipedia.org/wiki/Law_of_the_handicap_of_a_head_start).

prevent coercion and abuse. This also ensues from article 2 of the European Convention of Human Rights.

As sympathetic as it is to respond to people's need to decide for themselves how and when their lives end, this (how the aforementioned outer limits can be taken into account properly) is the challenge we all face.

Conclusion

In this contribution I have showed that there has been a development in thinking about the moral justification of euthanasia. The right to self-determination has had, and still has, a substantial impact on the law on euthanasia. In the process towards legalizing euthanasia in the Netherlands the right to self-determination initially was the driving force. Later the role of the principle of respect for autonomy was downplayed. The prevailing thought became that euthanasia is a matter of mercy. But the drive for more self-determination has always been there. Recently this has become more manifest. It is reported that within the framework of the law greater importance is given to the input and the perception of the patient. Furthermore, there are several initiatives that have been undertaken to increase the legal possibilities for euthanasia and assisted suicide.

About the author

Mr. dr. J.P. de Haan (jurdehaan@hotmail.com) is senior councilor at the Court of Justice 's-Hertogenbosch.

Work to Be Done: An Inquiry Concerning Legal Certainty in the Fourth Evaluation of the Dutch Euthanasia Act

Heleen Weyers[1]

Abstract

Legal certainty – that is predictability of law – is not just a legal principle but also an empirical topic. And as an empirical topic legal certainty can both be a goal and a means to achieve ends ('factual legal certainty'). As concerns the Termination of Life on Request and Assisted Suicide (Review Procedures) Act, these ends involve next to legal certainty, to promote social transparency and to guarantee the carefulness of ending life on request. In this article, it is argued that legal certainty has not been properly examined in the fourth evaluation of the Act. Therefore, the results that are offered by the evaluation cannot support the conclusion that the goal of legal certainty has been achieved. The article proposes to operationalize factual legal certainty as knowledge of the rules and being able to predict how the relevant government agencies will act. Such an operationalization of legal certainty has been used before (Marseille 1993). A comparison between Marseille's findings regarding legal certainty and what is known in this respect about euthanasia supposes that legal certainty regarding euthanasia law is to be expected. The conclusion is that an examination of legal certainty is possible ánd required.

Keywords: factual legal certainty, evaluation of law, operationalization, contextual factors.

---

[1] I thank Albert Klijn who put me on the right track; I would would like to thank Gijs van Donselaar for translating this article. I admire Govert den Hartogh for his high amount of very important contributions to Dutch discussion on euthanasia on almost all topics. To my knowledge, legal certainty is one of the few topics that escaped his attention.

Gijs van Donselaar, Peter Rijpkema, and Henri Wijsbek (eds), *The Ethics of Determining One's Own Death. Essays on Den Hartogh's What Kind of Death.*
Taylor & Francis Group, 2025
DOI: https://doi.org/10.5117/FEP2024.1.008.WEYE

Introduction

To secure legal certainty is one of the ends of the Termination of Life on Request and Assisted Suicide (Review Procedures) Act (hereafter for short: the Euthanasia Act). It is the end that is invariably mentioned first in the (now) four evaluations of the law. But reading these evaluations one learns alarmingly little about legal certainty in the empirical sense of that word. However, this article is not so much a complaint, as an effort to examine what could be done to learn more about legal certainty of physicians with regard to euthanasia and to stimulate this kind of research.

Legal Certainty and the Euthanasia Act

Legal Certainty: Principle of the Rechtsstaat

Legal certainty is a favorite topic among lawyers. It is one of the central principles of the *Rechtsstaat* (the continental form of the rule of law). Accordingly, professor of Administrative Law Michiel Scheltema, writes: "Law aims to bring certainty – therefore predictability – in the relations among people" (Scheltema 1989, p. 16).[2] Scheltema points out that it is not only the law that determines legal certainty, but that the institutions that apply the law also have a role to play. These have to function according to legal rules, see to it that the law's content is known by the citizens, take timely decisions, and meet expectations that have been raised. From a legal point of view it could be argued that if the law and the government agencies meet these requirements, legal certainty is realized.

---

2   Scheltema derives four requirements from the principle of legal certainty. In the first place, the requirement of legality, which implies that the government's conduct should have a legal base. Furthermore, the requirement that the law imposes such rules of conduct of the government that citizens will know what to expect from the government, the requirement that the fundamental rights of citizens will be circumscribed and secured, and finally the requirement of independent judiciary (Scheltema 1989, p. 16-17). It is evident that in legal fields other than administrative law the *Rechtsstaat* and its principles are sometimes appreciated differently, for instance, by prioritizing the legality requirement. But even then, the principal characteristic associated with legal certainty is predictability.

Factual Legal Certainty

If the legal quality is in order – that is citizens can predict the outcome of a procedure in principle – it does not follow *per se* that citizens can also do so in practice. To be able to do so, citizens should satisfy two conditions. On the one hand, they should know the rules: the citizen knows what she may and may not legally do (or what she is obliged to do). On the other hand, they must be able to predict how the relevant government agency will decide (Marseille 1993, p. 20). If both these conditions are satisfied, we can say there is *factual* legal certainty (the term stems from research by Marseille, 1993 and Oldenziel, 1998).[3]

The Function of Legal Certainty in the Euthanasia Act.

Those who have evaluated the Euthanasia Act mention legal certainty as one of the objectives of the Act. The other ends they mention, are social transparency and assuring carefulness of the practice of ending life on request.[4] A glance at the history of the Act's genesis reveals that legal certainty is an end of a distinct type, different from the other two (Weyers 2022, p. 249). The passing of the Euthanasia Act has a long prehistory (see Weyers 2002 esp. paragraphs 6.5; 7.3; 7.7; 8.1; 8.4; and 9.6; also for the references). Already 15 years before the Act was passed, case law had made it evident that doctors who complied with certain requirements of due care could count on being acquitted.[5] In their decisions, judges relied to a considerable degree on medical opinion and norms of medical ethics. That the patient should have

---

3   In the first evaluation of the Euthanasia Act, legal certainty is defined in a similar way: "Legal certainty is first and foremost about clarity of what applies legally and further about what can be expected regarding control, enforcement and sanction" (Onwuteaka-Philipsen et. al. 2007, p. 233). That it is not a legal matter but a empirical issue becomes clear from the subsequent sentence : "There is the more reason to examine the Euthanasia Act on this point, since an increase of legal certainty was explicitly one of the aims of the legislator. In aiming at certainty, she was not only considering the doctor, but also the patient." In the next evaluations of the Euthanasia Act, no further descriptions of legal certainty have been given.
4   The researchers of the third and fourth evaluation mention besides providing legal certainty, guaranteeing carefulness of ending life on request, and the promotion of transparency, a fourth aim: the provision of an accountability framework for doctors (Van der Heide et. al. 2023, p. 5). Under this heading they describe how often euthanasia is reported by doctors. Formerly, this was done under the heading of transparency.
5   The consideration was that the doctor was confronted with a conflict of duties (the doctor's duty to preserve life and her duty to relieve suffering). Such a situation may constitute a case of necessity (article 40 of the Penal Code). If judges accept an appeal to necessity, acquittal follows.

made a request[6] and that she should suffer gravely,[7] was uncontroversial. But it was less clear that a second doctor had to be involved and what the relation between the two doctors was allowed to be.[8]

In 1992, the then Medical Inspector, Gerrit van der Wal, concluded in his dissertation that the vast majority of the general practitioners adequately met the material requirements of due care (request and suffering), but that it was different for the procedural requirements. For instance, many doctors failed to notify the coroner that they had carried out euthanasia.[9] According to Van der Wal, they did not because they dreaded the emotional and practical burden of a judicial examination.[10]

Shortly after the research by Van der Wal, the first national research into the medical practice of termination of life was conducted. In this context, an instruction for the police was written at the request of the Royal Dutch Medical Association about how to proceed with notifications of euthanasia. Henceforth it should be done in a more discreet manner.[11] It was also clarified what information doctors had to submit. In other words, a notification procedure was established. The research revealed that doctors reported only eighteen percent of the cases of euthanasia. They indicated they did not want to be regarded as suspects of a criminal offence.

In 1994, the government decided to anchor this notification procedure by an Order in Council. This regulation was evaluated in 1996 in the context of the second survey of the medical practice of termination of life.[12] The percentage of notifications proved to have increased to 41. One fourth of the doctors and one out of six members of the magistracy said, without having been explicitly asked, that criminal review of euthanasia was out of place. Especially doctors had a preference for a review in advance by a colleague, possibly with a review afterwards. Only twenty percent of the doctors thought that the prosecutorial authorities should do the latter. A third of the responding groups saw a role for a non-criminal committee

6   This aligns with article 293 of the Penal Code where the termination of life on request is penalized. Otherwise it would be murder or manslaughter.
7   Otherwise there would be no role for the doctor.
8   Was a direct colleague permitted? A general practitioner in training? In 1984 the Royal Dutch Medical Association explicitly mentions the consultation requirement in its position statement. The association held that doctors should not consult a doctor in their own circle.
9   Failure to notify meant that the doctor had submitted a declaration of natural death. In case of euthanasia this is a false declaration which is penalized by article 228 of the Penal Code.
10 Van der Wal held that the criminal review of euthanasia was possibly counterproductive.
11 Especially police officers who showed up at consultation hours or drove up with screaming sirens were a thorn in the side of doctors.
12 Van der Wal and Van der Maas 1996.

to be played in this. In its response to the research, the government announced that the percentage of reporting had to increase. To that end, the cabinet resorted to a formerly formulated idea of having interdisciplinary composed committees as a buffer between the doctor and the prosecutorial authorities: the Regional Euthanasia Review Committees (hereafter for short: Review Committees). Their task at that moment (1998) was to review the notifications and to supply the prosecutorial authorities or the Inspectorate for Health Care with advice about the requirements for due care being met or not.

In 2001, the results of the third survey of the Dutch practice regarding medical behavior at the end of life was published. The percentage of notifications of euthanasia was found to have increased to 54. Just as in the research of Van der Wal, it was found in the national surveys that general practitioners in general complied with the requirements of due care (request and suffering). The problems with the procedural requirements (especially the consultation and notification) had declined in the course of the years.

Shortly before that research, in 1999, the government submitted a bill to change the criminal ban on termination of life on request: the Euthanasia Act. An exclusion from prosecution was introduced for doctors who reported euthanasia and complied with the requirements of due care.[13] At the same time, the position of the Review Committees was changed. If the doctor has complied with the requirements of due care, the case is closed. The prosecutorial authorities and the Inspectorate for Health Care were only to receive notification of cases in which, according to the Review Committees, the requirements of due care had not been met. This law entered into force in 2002.

That the requirements of due care potentially needed further specification was obvious from the parliamentary debate. Specifically, the requirement that the doctor should be convinced that the patient's suffering is unbearable, with no prospect of improvement, is interpreted as an open norm that can vary over time. The Review Committees therefore have the explicit task to provide a further specification of the requirements of careful practice

---

13   Under section 2 (1) of the Act, the physician must: a. be satisfied that the patient's request is voluntary and well considered; b. be satisfied that the patient's suffering is unbearable, with no prospect of improvement; c. have informed the patient about his situation and his prognosis; d. have come to the conclusion, together with the patient, that there is no reasonable alternative in the patient's situation; e. have consulted at least one other, independent physician, who must see the patient and give a written opinion on whether the due care criteria set out in (a) to (d) have been fulfilled; and f. have exercised due medical care and attention in terminating the patient's life or assisting in the patient's suicide.

when required.[14] In 2015, in response to earlier evaluations of the Act, the Review Committees have produced an overview of the way they interpret the requirements of due care. This is done in the *EuthanasiaCode,* several updates of which have now been published.[15] An example of such a further specification is that the situation of elderly people without severe conditions can constitute a case of unbearable suffering.

This short description shows that the legal history is characterized on the one hand by a clarification and the legal codification of the requirements of due care. And on the other, by changing the regime of control in a fashion that protects doctors to a considerable degree against criminal review. In other words: by providing more legal certainty, both as an end and as a means to attain social transparency and guaranteeing carefulness of ending life on request. Has legal certainty been achieved?

The Findings of the Empirical Survey about Legal Certainty in the Fourth Evaluation

It is remarkable that in the empirical part of the fourth evaluation of the Euthanasia Act the term 'legal certainty' is never mentioned.[16] Only in the concluding chapter it turns out that the researchers regard a part of the survey among doctors as an inquiry into legal certainty. It further turns out that in a part of the empirical research of the Review Committees, elements come to the fore that Scheltema counts as belonging to legal certainty (here too the term is omitted). Below, the survey of the activities of the Review Committees will be discussed and after that the survey among doctors.

The Fourth Evaluation: Research of the Review Committees
The evaluation research clarifies how the Review Committees act in regard to three elements that are mentioned by Scheltema (timeliness, conformity to law and meeting raised expectations).

The legally determined period within which the Review Committees have to send its findings to the doctor, is six weeks. In the research period (2017-2023) the Review Committees succeeded, but for the exception of

---

14 Therefore, the evaluations do not only look at the effects of the Act but also at the way the Review Committees specify the requirement of due care, therefore to the euthanasia law as a whole.

15 See for the most recent version: https://www.euthanasiecommissie.nl/euthanasiecode-2022/uitspraken/publicaties/ec-2022/ec-2022/7/5.

16 Neither is it in a substantive way in the legal part of the evaluation.

one year, to stay within the term of six weeks on the average (Van der Heide et. al. 2023, p. 175).[17] As regards conformity to law, the researchers have analyzed the annual reports of the Review Committees and a sample of reports of more complex cases.[18] From their analysis of the files they conclude that the *EuthanasiaCode* gives an accurate impression of the interpretation of the requirements of due care by the Review Committees and that there is but little difference between the *EuthanasiaCode* and what the Review Committees are actually doing (Van der Heide et. al. 2023, p. 201).

Furthermore, the researchers state that in general it is clear that if the doctor, the consultant and the possibly consulted expert[19] agree that the requirements of due care can be met, the Review Committee will rule accordingly (Van der Heide et. al. 2023, p. 201).

In other words, the evaluation shows that the Review Committees function as they are expect to do, given the three elements of legal certainty that were mentioned.[20]

The Fourth Evaluation: Research among Doctors

In the first evaluations of the Euthanasia Act, doctors were presented with the following statement: "Because of the Euthanasia Act, the legal certainty of doctors who perform euthanasia has improved." 74 percent of the doctors agreed with this statement; six percent disagreed (Onwuteaka-Philipsen et. al. 2007, p. 148).[21] A weakness of this method is that it is not obvious what doctors understand by legal certainty. As apparent from the conclusion, a different angle was chosen in the fourth evaluation:

---

17 If the Review Committee suspects that the doctor has not complied with the due care criteria, the term is almost always longer. This is because in that case there is always a meeting with the doctor, and an internal consultation. The most important reason for failures of staying within the deadline is in general that the Review Committees cannot– temporarily – manage the ever increasing number of reports.

18 Reports of euthanasia for patients with dementia, with mental disorders or with an accumulation of old-age conditions.

19 In some more complex cases, for example a patient with a psychiatric disorder asking euthanasia, an expert has to be consulted by the doctor.

20 The prosecutorial authorities and the Inspectorate of Health Care have not been investigated in this way. For them, euthanasia is only one of their subjects and a subject that they hardly ever have to deal with. The latter is explained by the fact that the Review Committees decide that the doctor has complied with the due care criteria in almost all cases.

21 It is not clear if the statement was used in the second and third evaluation, but the researchers did conclude that the Euthanasia Act contributes to the three ends, alternatively that they are realized (Van der Heide et. al. 2012, p. 15; Onwuteaka-Philipsen et. al. 2017, p. 253).

Concerning the legal certainty for doctors, it was found that 82 percent of the Dutch doctors would be willing to perform euthanasia under the present regulation, or to assist in suicide. Fear of review and its consequences is rarely a reason to decline a request for the termination of life. This shows that doctors seem to experience a sufficient degree of legal certainty about their life-ending actions on request (Van der Heide et. al. 2023, p. 287).

The researchers have determined the willingness to perform euthanasia by the summation of the percentage of doctors who have ever carried out euthanasia and the percentage of doctors who are willing to do so. In 2022 the first group consisted of 55 percent of the doctors, and the second group of 27 percent. In the aggregate that amounts to the 82 percent mentioned.

It is interesting that the researchers not only record the percentages of 2022 but also those of the earlier occasions on which similar research was conducted.

	2022 %	2016 %	2011 %	2005 %	2001 %	1995 %	1990 %
ever	55	57	60	51	57	53	54
conceivably	27	24	25	33	32	35	34
aggregate	82	81	85	84	89	88	88

This table (Van der Heide et. al. 2023, p. 140) shows a problematic finding concerning legal certainty. The assumption was that the Euthanasia Act would offer more legal certainty. Yet the percentages concerning willingness have remained approximately the same from 1990 onwards. The logical conclusion would then be that the Euthanasia Act has not exerted the expected influence upon legal certainty among doctors.

But probably something else is going on, namely that willingness is not a reliable indicator of legal certainty. Among other things this is clear from the quotes cited following the table. In the first quote a relation with legal certainty is conceivable: "The criteria of due care are of great help to me." (Van der Heide et. al. 2023, p. 140). But in the second, something else seems to be in play: "I think, most important of all is a certain conviction I get. So it is really a certain conviction within me, a certain sense that I am not going to abandon that patient." (Van der Heide et. al. 2023, p. 140) From earlier research it is also clear that doctors let their personal opinions – that it is important that the patient solves her personal conflicts first for instance – determine their willingness to perform euthanasia (Ten Cate 2019).[22] In the evaluation, the doctors also mention a number of factors which may reduce their willingness to comply with a request for euthanasia, like pressure from the patients or a long life expectancy (Van der Heide et. al. 2023, p. 41). In other words, one cannot read the willingness to apply euthanasia as a one to one fit with sufficient legal certainty.

That the researchers were not concerned with legal certainty is further manifested by the fact that they do not give an interpretation of the difference in the willingness between doctor- and patient groups in this light. It is clear that willingness is highest among general practitioners and much lower among medical specialists and nursing home doctors (nowadays called specialists in geriatric medicine).[23] It is also clear that the willingness to perform euthanasia is highest with patients who have cancer. It is much lower with people who suffer from a psychiatric condition and with people in an advanced stage of dementia who do not suffer from any additional grave conditions.[24] Is something amiss with the legal certainty of doctors in these situations?

The second element that is indicated by the researchers in the conclusion – fear of review and consequences – is an accidental finding. Of the 746 doctors who were involved in the research, 170 submitted an answer to the open question: "Into what limits did you run when you refused a request for euthanasia that satisfied the requirements of due care?"

Four percent of these doctors mentioned: "fear of review and consequences" (Van der Heide et. al. 2023, p. 143).[25]

The conclusion from this analysis can be no other than that legal certainty has not been researched systematically and properly in the fourth evaluation (nor in any of the three earlier ones) and that therefore the researchers offer no support for the statement that this end has been achieved.[26]

---

22 See for critical remarks on personal opinions of doctors regarding requirements of due care Den Hartogh 2023, p 225.
23 General practitioners: 90 percent; medical specialists: 70 percent; specialists in geriatric medicine: 72 percent (Van der Heide et. al. 2023, p. 140).
24 For general practitioners it is respectively 90 percent; 44 percent and 32 percent (Van der Heide et. al. 2023, p. 149).
25 In earlier evaluations this reason was not reported.
26 Needless to say, the thesis is not that legal certainty has not been achieved, only that it does not follow from the findings that are presented that it has.

There is Information about the first Condition: Knowledge of the Rules

Assuming that factual legal certainty has two conditions – knowledge of the rules and knowing how relevant government agencies reach decisions – it makes sense to survey what doctors know about the Euthanasia Act and about the review procedure. There was no such survey in the fourth evaluation. Earlier, however, the first condition has been researched.

In 1996 the researchers concluded that almost all doctors are acquainted with the existence of requirements of due care and that they were able to cite several of them (Van der Wal and Van der Maas 1996, p. 157-158). Furthermore, four multiple choice questions about knowledge of the Act were posed in the first evaluation (Onwuteaka-Philipsen et. al. 2007). Two of those were answered correctly by about two thirds of the doctors;[27] the other two questions by less than half. The latter two questions concerned more special cases like euthanasia for incompetent patients with an advance directive and for minors.[28] A relatively large percentage of doctors furthermore indicate that they do not know the answer to these two questions.[29]

Although the answers do not testify to a thorough knowledge of the rules, it has not been researched since 2007 within the context of the evaluation of the Euthanasia Act. It was, however, researched in the so-called KOPPEL-research (Van Delden et. al. 2011).[30] In the quantitative section of that survey, five multiple choice questions were posed. Regrettably not the two questions that were found to be difficult in the evaluation of 2007. It turned out that at least eighty percent of the doctors answered four questions correctly (Van Delden et. al. 2011, p. 71).[31] The exception regards a question about a referral obligation; 80 percent of the doctors wrongly thought there was such an legal obligation.

---

27 Euthanasia is only permitted in the terminal stage – 69 percent answered correctly that this is not the case; the consultant should be a doctor, affiliated with Support and Consultation Euthanasia the Netherlands (SCEN) – 66 percent answered correctly that this is not the case (Onwuteaka-Philipsen et. al. 2007, p. 149).
28 The question about the advance directive was answered correctly by 40 percent – euthanasia is allowed in such cases; the question about the minor by 35 percent – euthanasia is allowed in such cases (Onwuteaka-Philipsen et. al. 2007, 149). Incidentally, nearly all doctors – 92 percent -thought they were sufficiently informed about the content of the Euthanasia Act (Onwuteaka-Philipsen et. al. 2007, p. 148).
29 20 percent in the case of dementia and 40 percent in the case of euthanasia for minors.
30 A research into knowledge and opinions of the general public and medical professionals regarding medical decision making and treatment at the end of life.
31 The answer "I do not know" was given by about five percent of the doctors.

Furthermore, it was found from the presentation of short cases and the answering of questions about it, that 58 percent of the doctors wrongly thought that euthanasia is not permitted in cases of chronic depression; thirty percent indicated not to know. Furthermore 59 percent thought – wrongly – that it was not permitted in early stages of dementia; 23 percent indicated not to know (Van Delden et. al. 2011, p. 83). This research, too, therefore demonstrates that knowledge of euthanasia in more complex cases is poorer than of euthanasia for a patient who suffers from for example cancer.[32]

In the qualitative section of the Koppel-research it was found that the 49 doctors who were interviewed were well-informed about the requirements of due care of the Euthanasia Act. They were able to reproduce them during the interviews and often used the literal wordings from the Euthanasia Act (Van Delden et. al. 2011, p. 158). If asked, they also gave the right interpretations of them. Yet here too, some lack of knowledge surfaced. Doctors know the criterion of severe suffering but a number of them give a narrower interpretation of it than is prescribed by the euthanasia law. Some of them for instance, think that the patient should be in the terminal phase (Van Delden et. al. 2011, p. 216).

So, doctors seem to have quite some knowledge about what the rules dictate in 'normal' cases of euthanasia.[33] This is less so in the more complex cases. This is also the conclusion of the first evaluation of the Euthanasia Act:

> The notification and review system works in a predictable way in most cases and is also experienced as such by doctors and their organizations. ... In borderline cases legal certainty is less established (Onwuteaka-Philipsen et al. 2007, p. 26).

What doctors know about the review procedure has never been surveyed. Researchers do ask questions about experience with the review procedure, but not in terms of knowledge of what the Review Committees will do.[34]

---

32   Euthanasia for patients with cancer is the most common case. For example In 2021 61.1 percent of the notifications were of cases of incurable cancer. Conditions of the nervous system, heart – and vascular conditions and lung conditions were less frequent: in the aggregate 14.2 percent of the reports. Euthanasia for people with dementia or psychiatric conditions were even less frequent. The Review Committees report them in numbers: 215 (of whom 6 in an advanced stage of dementia) and 115 respectively. (https://www.euthanasiecommissie.nl/actueel/nieuws/2022/03/31/jaarverslag-2021)

33   Den Hartogh's interest in knowledge of doctors with respect to euthanasia law is clear from Den Hartogh 2023, section 12.2.

34   Answer categories regarding the question: "How did you experience the review procedure?" are: neutral; time consuming; burdensome; relieving; supporting; clarifying; invading privacy

Summary

It has been clarified that factual legal certainty plays an important part in achieving societal transparency regarding euthanasia and a careful euthanasia practice. Furthermore, that factual legal certainty has never been adequately operationalized in the evaluations and therefore neither systematically researched. It follows that the conclusion that the end of legal certainty has been achieved is unsupported.

It was argued that factual legal certainty is about being able to predict what decision will be reached by the decision-making agencies. For this, two conditions are mentioned: knowledge of the relevant rules and of the functioning of those agencies.[35] Only with respect to the first condition something is known regarding doctors and euthanasia. The data should be interpreted with some caution because only a restricted number of questions were asked. It seems that doctors know the rules regarding so-called 'standard cases' of euthanasia. But this is less so with respect to more complex cases.

Can a Step Forward be Taken?

In the foregoing it has been clarified that little is known about legal certainty regarding the euthanasia law. In what follows, an attempt to take a further step is made by taking recourse to an earlier study and to a comparison between the situation of the respondents of that study and the situation of doctors with regard to euthanasia.

An Inspiring Example

In 1993, Bert Marseille, an expert in public administration, examined the two conditions that are important for factual legal certainty (Marseille 1993). Marseille observed that the knowledge of respondents (people on two distinct employment benefit schemes who were looking for permission for further training) about his five questions was rather diverse.[36] And he too found that two questions were poorly answered.

In contrast to the euthanasia researchers, Marseille reflected on his findings. He noticed differences between his two research groups and

---

and incriminating (Van der Heide et. al. 2023, p. 168).
35   What is at stake is not perfect knowledge, but knowledge sufficient for prediction.
36   He posed seven questions two of which he did not report about, due to methodological problems (Marseille 1993, p. 196).

observed that for three questions these differences were negligible. But precisely for the two questions that were answered less well, the difference in knowledge was largest.[37] He also checked if there was a relation between the ways in which the respondents answered the several questions. That proved hardly to be the case. In other words, the answers do not provide a general impression of the knowledge but only an indication of the knowledge of the respondents of that one aspect.[38] That is that he had to conclude that there was no overall knowledge on the rules, only knowledge of separate topics.

Marseille also asked questions about factors that have an influence on knowledge about rights and duties. Among other things he looked into what he calls "sources of knowledge". In his research: the employment office, the social service, the law, written information, knowing someone in the same position and one's own estimation of what will be the case.[39] He found that the employment office and the benefits agency were the most important sources of knowledge. Besides, "one's own estimation" was quite frequently mentioned. And, unsurprisingly, it was found that consulting the employment office as a source, correlated positively with knowledge, and relying on one's own estimation, negatively (Marseille 1993, p. 202).

Marseille also examined the ability to predict the decision of the benefits agency. He asked the interviewed benefit recipients how probable they thought it was that they would be permitted to attend a training, and also if the employment office had told them anything about it (Marseille 1993, p. 209-210). It became clear that the employment office was more pessimistic about the permission than the recipients. It was furthermore found that receiving information from the employment office positively affected the ability of benefit receivers to predict the decision of the benefit agency. Marseille found no correlation between knowledge of the rules and the ability to adequately estimate the probability of permission for training (Marseille 1993, p. 213).

Marseille's research is inspiring for various reasons. He demonstrates that research into the two conditions of legal certainty is possible. He indicates that there are difficulties in determining knowledge of the rules. He is attentive to the resources for the predictability of the acts of the government agency. And he was able to say something about the relative weight of the two conditions.

---

37 He gave a further analysis of this, but that need not concern us for now.
38 He was able to make an index which clarified how many of the five questions were answered correctly by the several respondents, but this index could not be shown to represent a uniform scale (Marseille 1993, p. 196-199). That is there is no statistical coherence between the answers.
39 The latter is not a real source of knowledge (Marseille 1993, p. 202).

Three Differences that are Important for Factual Legal Certainty

Marseille's research is also relevant because it enables us to indicate a number of relevant differences in respect to legal certainty between on the one hand the situation of benefit recipients who want further training and on the other doctors who carry out euthanasia.

Self-regulation

The rules Marseille asked the benefit recipients about, were rules that were imposed on benefit recipients and benefit agencies by the legislator. This is quite different for the rules regarding euthanasia. Those rules are to a high degree the result of self-regulation (Griffiths 2000). In as far as they were not (especially consultation and reporting), the Royal Dutch Medical Association turned these rules into her own rules.[40] This means that doctors have many sources for their knowledge of the rules of due care and reporting. They are socialized in these rules. Their own organizations ensure in various ways that doctors are regularly confronted with the rules (articles in medical journals, trainings, intervision groups, conferences, position statements). Doctors can also turn to their organizations if they want information about the rules for euthanasia.[41]

The Presence of a Script

In the qualitative section of the aforementioned KOPPEL-survey, doctors were found to structure their stories about euthanasia according to the requirements of due care. They employ what in professional terms is called a 'script': "a set of expectations about what will happen next in a well-understood situation" (Schank and Abelson 1995, p. 5). Although scripts usually remain implicit, people use them continuously. Thanks to scripts they know how to act and what to expect of others. People learn scripts from concrete practical experiences and hearing stories of others about that situation. The integration of experiences and stories renders so-called 'functional knowledge'. "Understanding means mapping your stories onto my stories" (Schank and Abelson 1995, p. 16). Characteristic for scripts is that one need not tell everything, but that some elements are so essential that they cannot be left out. For doctors, with regard to euthanasia the essential

---

40 By now, there is also a number of directives that doctor should obey that are also part of the assessment by the Review Committees (for example about the medically responsible application).
41 Doctors can also find a lot of information about the rules and the way that the Review Committees reach their decisions on the websites of the Royal Dutch Medical Association and the Review Committees. Quite some doctors (53 percent) have experience with euthanasia and review.

elements appear to be the requirements of due care. In structuring their experiences along the line of the due care criteria they show their knowledge of the rules in their stories.

It is an open question whether there is also a script in Marseille's case of an education for benefit recipients. What is expected of a benefit recipient who wants additional training? Whatever the answer, Marseille did not ask. The only question that concerned such expectations, was about the handing in of a job slip. This is what is called 'shallow knowledge' (Weyers and Van Tol 2014): knowledge of bare facts.[42]

Advanced Review
For the ability to predict the result of the assessment, the employment office played an important part. Regarding the Euthanasia Act, that part is played by an independent consultant. Their consultation is also called advanced review. In almost all cases, the consultant is a doctor who is affiliated with Support and Consultation Euthanasia in the Netherlands. These doctors have received special training and participate in intervision groups. They are, then, experts in the rules of the euthanasia law and in general they are very experienced with the rules surrounding euthanasia. They should be able to predict what the Review Committee will do. In the vast majority of the notifications, the independent consultant thinks that the requirements of due care have been satisfied and the Review Committee concur. Thus the review system has a built-in element that provides doctors with an almost hundred percent certainty about the prediction of the result.

Research into the Legal Certainty with Regard to the euthanasia law is Very Much Wanted.

The difference between the situations of benefit recipients and doctors shows that the circumstances for factual legal certainty of doctors are quite favorable. If research would show that doctors have functional knowledge of the law and can predict (with help from an independent consultant) the judgment of the Review Committees, it will not come as a big surprise. Why then still urge for research on the legal certainty of doctors who (want to) carry out euthanasia?

---

42 Schank and Abelson (cognition scientists) are convinced that such knowledge is not helpful in daily life. At most It serves to make an impression (Schank and Abelson 1995, p. 11).

Promises are Promises

The purpose of the evaluation is to inquire whether the goals of the Euthanasia Act have been achieved, and that includes legal certainty. All the more so since, ZonMw[43], the organization that commissioned the research, considers legal certainty as an element that may not be omitted in an evaluation of a law.[44] It is remarkable that there are nonetheless hardly any evaluations on the website of ZonMw that involve research of legal certainty. And where they do, the findings are not supported in the manner of Marseille.[45] Other operationalizations of legal certainty are lacking as well. In that sense the researchers of the fourth evaluation should be praised because they at least made an effort.

More Clarity about 'Complex Requests'

It is not really clear why doctors answer questions about complex situations less well. It would be good to clarify if this has to do with legal certainty or if other factors play a part. It is especially desirable that problems with legal certainty are treated independently from other aspects that determine willingness.[46]

A Frequently Used Means

That we know so little about the existence of factual legal certainty is the more regrettable since legal certainty is an object of concern with many laws. On the terrain of ZonMw one can think of the Organ Donation Act,

---

43 ZonMw is a financing organization for innovation and research in healthcare. The evaluations of the Euthanasia Act and the KOPPEL-study, for example, are financed by ZonMW.

44 https://www.zonmw.nl/sites/zonmw/files/typo3-migrated-files/Brochure_Evaluatie_Regelgeving.pdf: p. 4.

45 The interpretation discussed here, is cognitive in nature. Arguably, factual legal certainty may have a subjective element. The researchers of the evaluations write about "experiencing" legal certainty (Van der Heide et. al. 2023, p. 287). Criminologist Marijke Malsch includes research such as that of Marseille under "objective" certainty. In addition, she distinguished "subjective" certainty. To identify the latter kind of certainty she asked her respondents to indicate how certain they were about the correctness of their answers to factual questions (Malsch 1989, p. 126).

46 The more so since doctors are permitted to carry out euthanasia, yet have no obligation to do so. A doctor may have good reasons for refraining from carrying out, but if she refrains because she is insufficiently certain of her legal position, evaluation research should bring this to light. The (further) unraveling of willingness should also pay attention to another indispensable element in a law evaluation: research into side effects (such as patients who do not receive the desired euthanasia because euthanasia law does not provide sufficient factual legal certainty after all for doctors confronted with 'complex cases'). So far, there has been no systematic attention in the evaluations of the Euthanasia Act for this either.

the Medical Research Involving Human Subjects Act, the Embryo Act or the Compulsory Mental Healthcare Act, to mention just a couple. Knowledge about legal certainty as a means would serve to advance beyond the mere determination that an end has been achieved. It could lead to an explanation as to why the end was achieved (or not).[47]

There is Room
Up until now, legal certainty has been neglected in the evaluations of the Euthanasia Act. It is high time to make room for it. That room now exists. So far, it has been researched seven times if doctors report euthanasia.[48] And though researchers suggest that doctors have failed to report one fifth of the cases since 2002 – see for instance the reporting percentage of 82 in 2021 (Van der Heide et. al. 2023, p. 287)[49] – they also show that if a doctor thinks that it is a case of euthanasia,[50] she will report it as such.[51] That implies a reporting percentage of nearly a hundred. That is a good result, but it is pointless to establish it time and again when nothing special is going on. A rejoinder could be that in this way it is not known what percentage of the total number of deaths consists of cases of euthanasia. For that, one could use the percentage that is reported by the Review Committees every year. It is a rather crude method of measurement, but the question is how bad that is.[52] Furthermore, it is clear that the research into due care strongly leans on the judgements of the Review Committees. What the researchers report is actually a repetition of what the committees' annual reports say. In other words: less attention for the goals of transparency and due care; a lot more attention to factual legal certainty. It is possible! It is required!

---

47 This goes beyond the usual assignment of a law evaluation (effectiveness and side-effects). But if it is found that the goal of legal certainty is insufficiently achieved, then the question as to why that is so naturally emerges.
48 The way in which the research is conducted has been criticized from the beginning. The core of that criticism is that in the research it cannot be clarified if the termination of life was not a side-effect of medically indicated pain relief and should therefore fall under the head of regular medical treatment.
49 Den Hartogh (2003) was the first scholar to criticize the researchers on this.
50 There is then a strong relation with the means that are employed – muscle relaxants and/or barbiturates – and consultation of an independent doctor (Van der Heide et. al. 2023, p. 165-166). In the three earlier evaluations it is also reported that if a doctor regards the termination of life as euthanasia, she will inform the coroner (among others Onwuteaka-Philipsen et. al. 2007, p. 178).
51 See for an elaboration on this Den Hartogh 2023, section 10.6.
52 For 2021, the researchers arrive at a percentage of 5.4 of all deaths (taking the criticism of the calculation into account, that percentage is too high); The Review Committees at 4.5 percent.

About the author

Heleen Weyers (h.a.m.weyers@rug.nl) is a former assistant professor in legal theory at the University of Groningen. She writes about euthanasia and law since 1996. Her latest publication concerns the developments regarding the Dutch euthanasia law since the enactment of the law in 2002.

Literature

Delden, J.J.M. et. al., *Kennis en opvattingen van publiek en professionals over medische besluitvorming en behandeling rond het einde van het leven. Het KOPPEL-onderzoek,* Den Haag: ZonMW 2011.

Griffiths, John, "Self-Regulation by the Dutch Medical Profession of Medical Behavior that Potentially Shortens Life", pp. 173-191, in: Hans Krabbendam and Hans-Martien ten Napel (eds), *Regulating Morality: A Comparison of the Role of the State in Mastering the Mores in the Netherlands and the United States,* Antwerpen-Apeldoorn: Maclu, 2000.

Hartogh, Govert den, "Mysterieuze cijfers: meldingspercentage van euthanasie kan niet meer stijgen", *Medisch Contact* 2003: pp 1063-1066.

Hartogh, Govert den, *What kind of death: the ethics of determining one's own death,* New York: Routledge, 2023.

Heide, Agnes van der et.al., *Tweede evaluatie. Wet toetsing levensbeëindiging op verzoek en hulp bij zelfdoding,* Den Haag: ZonMw, 2007.

Heide. Agnes van der e.a., *Vierde evaluatie. Wet toetsing levensbeëindiging op verzoek en hulp bij zelfdoding,* Den Haag: ZonMw, 2023.

Malsch, Marijke, *Lawyers' Predictions of Judicial Decisions: A Study on Calibration of Experts,* Dissertation Rijksuniversiteit Leiden 1989.

Marseille, A.T., *Voorspelbaarheid van bestuurshandelen, Een onderzoek naar rechtsregels en beslissingen over het volgen van scholing met behoud van uitkering,* Deventer: Kluwer, 1993.

Oldenziel, H.A., *Wetgeving en rechtszekerheid. Een onderzoek naar de bijdrage van het legaliteitsvereiste aan de rechtszekerheid van de burger,* Deventer: Kluwer, 1998.

Onwuteaka-Philipsen, B.D., et. al., *Wet toetsing levensbeëindiging op verzoek en hulp bij zelfdoding,* Den Haag: ZonMw, 2007.

Onwuteaka-Philipsen, B.D. et. al., *Wet toetsing levensbeëindiging op verzoek en hulp bij zelfdoding,* Den Haag: ZonMw, 2017.

Schank, Roger C. and Robert P. Abelson, "Knowledge and Memory: The Real Story", pp. 1-86, in: Robert S. Wyer Jr. (ed), *Knowledge and Memory: the Real Story',* Hillsdale, New Jersey: Lawrence Erlbaum Associates Publ. 1995.

Scheltema, M., "De rechtsstaat", pp. 11-27, in: J.W.M. Engels et. al. (red.), *De rechtsstaat herdacht,* Zwolle: W.E.J. Tjeenk Willink, 1989.

Wal, G. van der, *Euthanasie en hulp bij zelfdoding door huisartsen,* Rotterdam: WYT Uitgeefgroep, 1992.

Wal, G. van der and P.J. van der Maas, *Euthanasie en andere medische beslissingen rond het levenseinde. De praktijk en de meldingsprocedure,* Den Haag: Sdu Uitgevers, 1996.

Weyers, Heleen, *Euthanasie. Het proces van rechtsverandering,* Dissertatie Rijksuniversiteit Groningen 2002.

Weyers, Heleen, *Euthanasie in Nederland 2002-2022,* Den Haag: Boomjuridisch, 2022.

Weyers Heleen and Donald van Tol, "Scripts, de voertuigen van kennis", *Recht der Werkelijkheid* 2014 (2) 24-50.

Fear, Incompetence and Death. Empirical Observations and Ethical Concerns about Dying with Advanced Dementia

Eva C. A. Asscher

Abstract

In Den Hartogh's *What Kind of Death. The Ethics of Determining One's Own Death* (2023) a thorough philosophical analysis of the ethical considerations on suicide and other means of determining one's own death is based on the empirical evidence published on the topic. In this contribution I want to emphasise the importance of concerns arising from the practice, and attempt to add to the analysis in his book by posing a number of questions arising from that practice. In order to so, I first elucidate a few empirical observations, some of which are well-known, others are just emerging. First, the fear of review and the possibility of legal sanctions physicians experience when contemplating active ending of life, particularly in 'difficult cases', including cases in which the patient is incompetent and thus unable to ask for active ending of life himself. Second, the on-going increase of continuous palliative sedation from 8% of all deaths in 2005 to 23% in 2021. (Van der Heide et al 2023, p.17) Taken together, these observations raise the question whether they might be related. It is clear that active ending of life for patients with advanced dementia is very difficult to obtain in the Netherlands, and it is equally clear that some of these patients are suffering. It is important to consider and research the practice and decision-making for continuous palliative sedation in these patients and how this practice should be evaluated ethically. The two questions I would like to highlight here are, first: how should we understand relatively early continuous palliative sedation in patients with advanced dementia and, second: what risks may arise from such a practice?

Gijs van Donselaar, Peter Rijpkema, and Henri Wijsbek (eds), *The Ethics of Determining One's Own Death. Essays on Den Hartogh's What Kind of Death.*
Taylor & Francis Group, 2025
DOI: https://doi.org/10.5117/FEP2024.1.009.ASSC

Keywords: review, legal sanctions, due care criteria, palliative sedation, advance directive, dementia.

Introduction

Empirical research and a thorough familiarity with a practice can further philosophical analysis, as Den Hartogh clearly shows in *What Kind of Death. The Ethics of Determining One's Own Death.*(2023) Empirical data can inform normative reasoning in a number of ways. Most prominent in the book is the following: when arguments against allowing a practice are based on hypothetical existence of an undesirable outcome, it is essential to discover whether this outcome is indeed present. For instance, theoretical concerns that are raised before the introduction of a regulation on medical aid in dying, can often only be tested by close observation of the developing practice. One concern is that introduction of medical aid in dying is a step on a "slippery slope". This slippery slope implies that if active-ending-of-life is permitted in some but not in other cases, this will change under the pressure of practice, and more and more cases will be permitted and performed. Another example is the risk of misuse. These concerns can only be tested by empirical studies of active ending of life in practice. As Den Hartogh argues, the risks of misuse of active ending of life in settings which are highly regulated are much smaller, than the risks of misuse in normal end-of-life practices. (p. 202) For physicians intending to kill someone, it is easier to abuse other options (such as undesired or not indicated stopping of life supporting treatment), which are less scrutinised.

Empirical research, therefore, is invaluable in addressing certain theoretical concerns. However, some would argue closeness to practice and empirical research may uncover new questions or situations that are unforeseen. It is then sometimes necessary to evaluate those new questions and that can reignite old debates.

In this paper, I highlight some recent empirical findings that I will argue compel us to re-evaluate some of the questions related to the end-of-life practice, and to consider some new ethical concerns. The normative presuppositions that make these developments morally relevant are that active ending of life is a practice that can only be justified when it is well regulated and transparent in order to avoid abuse.

Before exploring the empirical findings from practice and their ethical consideration, it may be helpful to set the scene with a brief summary of the ethical and legal context of active ending of life.

The Dutch context

In the Netherlands euthanasia has been legalised since 2002, when the Termination of Life on Request and Assisted Suicide (Review Procedures) Act came into force. Earlier both euthanasia and assisted suicide were forbidden and punishable under the criminal law. The Act formerly allows physicians to perform euthanasia and assisted suicide (henceforth euthanasia) by codifying an exception to the criminal code provided the physician complies with the due care criteria and notifies the review committees of the euthanasia. If the review committees judge that a euthanasia is performed with due care, the case is closed and not sent on to the public prosecution. The Dutch law also allows for euthanasia based on an advance euthanasia directive (AED), for instance in cases of advanced dementia. This provision is the only part of the law not based on case law at the time of the enactment and (has been) is considered morally controversial.(Hertogh 2007)

In practice, euthanasia performed on patients with advanced dementia based on an advance euthanasia directive is rare. For instance, in 2022 only six cases of euthanasia on incompetent patients with advanced dementia were performed and reported to the review committees out of a total of 8720 cases of euthanasia in the Netherlands that year (RTE 2022). This is in contrast with a much higher number of advanced directives likely to circulate in the population. A patient advocate organisation estimates that 21% of the population has an advance directive 55% of which contains a request for euthanasia. (Harnas and Toersen 2018, p. 5) The group of respondents was not entirely representative of the Dutch population, being somewhat older (in age) and higher educated (p. 4), this bias might have caused an overrepresentation of people with an advance (euthanasia) directive as both these characteristics correspond with a higher likelihood of a written AED (p. 7). The main reason respondents gave in this questionnaire for making an advance euthanasia directive was to avoid ending like a "glasshouse plant" (vegetable) (91%), the second was to avoid losing independence. (p. 11)

In the context of an ageing population this becomes more important: for instance in the Netherlands the number of people over 65 is increasing absolutely (and relatively), with the expectation of 4.8 million people over 65 in 2040.(Stoeldraijer et al 2017, p. 5) Age of course, is the single largest predictor of the development of dementia, which is currently untreatable. (Ott 1996, Kivipelto 2006, Soria Lopez 2019) If this does not change in the near future, we will see more people with (early-stage) dementia. Some of these people will have an advance euthanasia directive and hope to be spared the later stages of dementia. But in all likelihood very few of them will be granted euthanasia.

Some empirical observations 1: physicians' reluctance to perform euthanasia

In the past, physicians' reluctance to perform euthanasia in so-called difficult cases has been studied. The reasons they gave with respect to advanced dementia were that they are uncertain about the fulfilment of the due care criteria, that they have a strong preference for performing euthanasia when the patient can still confirm the wish orally and competently, and their own personal, moral boundaries.(Bolt et al 2015) This corresponds to Den Hartogh's description of assisted suicide in the Benelux-countries as the joint act of ending the patient's life.(Den Hartogh 2023, p. 84) One could argue that something similar happens in euthanasia, the physician and patient grow together towards the conclusion that the active ending of the patient's life is the best and only remaining option to relieve their suffering. In this context it is understandable that the act of ending the life of a no longer competent patient, whereby this joint responsibility and development is not possible, is more difficult.

The second concern: the uncertainty about fulfilling the due care criteria might mean different things. While the case of doctor Arends (Supreme Court 2020) was on-going, one study confirmed this uncertainty in general practitioners (GPs), maybe confusion, about the fulfilment of the due care criteria in cases of euthanasia in a patient with advanced dementia.(Schuurman et al 2021) Moreover, the case was widely publicised and discussed in the popular media, including an advertisement condemning euthanasia on patients who are no longer competent.(Kleijne 2017) However, since then the Supreme Court has passed judgment on the case and has thus clarified the criteria for performing euthanasia (Supreme Court 2020) and a number of commentators have discussed the strengths and weaknesses of this judgment.(Den Hartogh 2021, Rozemond 2021) The regional review committees and the Royal Dutch Medical Association have both produced updated guidelines in order to clarify the criteria and steps necessary to perform euthanasia with due care in these cases.(RTE 2022, KNMG 2021)

Even with these clarifications the concern about knowing and meeting the due care criteria might still persist. This concern might be an accurate description of the (in)ability of individual physicians to be confident about the content of the guidelines, especially for those physicians not regularly engaging with euthanasia for patients with advanced dementia. Second, it might refer to the remaining open ends of the Supreme Court verdict such as what qualifies as resistance in the patient with advanced dementia, which should be taken seriously and may preclude performance of euthanasia. Concerns about the remaining unclarity might worry those physicians who have been following the legal and ethical debate closely. Third, it might concern the fear of failing to fulfil the due care criteria, which is supported by the following empirical observations. This fear exists over and above the concerns mentioned before.

The following empirical observations on fear of review and prosecution are still tentative. They rely on different sources: either on relatively robust interview and questionnaire data from a slightly different but related situation, or on observations directly applicable to the question I want to raise but less scientifically sound. Taken together I would argue that they are sufficient to develop my working hypothesis.

In the Netherlands, there is a regulation which allows physicians to end the life of newborn infants (younger than 1 year old) (to have their life ended actively) if the physician fulfils a number of due care criteria.(Regeling 2015) The similarities with euthanasia in patients with dementia on the basis of an advance euthanasia directive, lie therein that the patient is not competent to request the active ending of life and therefore the decision cannot be conceived of as a joint action. An important difference is that the patient never has been competent in these cases and the decision is made together with the parents (parental consent is one of the criteria). In cases based on an AED, the former wish of the patient is known and no consent of the family or other representative is necessary. This regulation for active ending of life in newborns is not a formal law and all cases are forwarded to the prosecutorial authorities, unlike those cases of euthanasia judged to fulfil the due care criteria. (Regeling 2015) This regulation is very rarely invoked, with one reported case between 2016 and 2021. In an interview study, physicians ascribed their hesitancy to perform active ending of life on a newborn first and foremost to the fear of review and prosecution. (Ploem et al 2022, p. 126) This fear was increased as a result of the publicity of the prosecution of doctor Arends, and some physicians referred to her case as a deterrent. (Ploem p. 115)

Directly relevant data, though not from formal research, can be gathered from the cases GPs-in-training present in the classroom. The students are asked to identify a case they have been worried or unsure about and to discuss the ethical aspects in a learning environment. Of course these cases remain anonymous and cannot be reported on fully. However, requests for euthanasia once people have (advanced) dementia is a recurring theme. The fear of review is really notable and features frequently. Sometimes physicians experience waiting for the first (and if all due care criteria are met, final) judgement of the review committees as burdensome. Pending the decision of the committee, while the physician is still uncertain about the outcome of the first review, they worry about further legal consequences and possible criminal prosecution.

I would hypothesise that in practice, this fear of review and prosecution is an underreported but important reason to avoid active ending of life , and particularly in the complex cases where patients are not competent.

It is important to note that this fear is not rationally justifiable in the case of euthanasia, if one considers the numbers of physicians that have actually had to face the prosecutionary authorities. In the past years, the numbers of performed cases of euthanasia that were judged as not fulfilling the due care criteria are very low: in 2021 (0,09% of total number of performed cases), 13 in 2022 (0,15%). All cases that are not judged as performed with due care are forwarded to both the criminal prosecution and the inspectorate for health. Most cases are being either considered by the inspectorate or the criminal prosecution, and most are dismissed before a case is brought. There has been one criminal prosecution, where the physician was acquitted. There have been several cases considered by the inspectorate for health, some of which have let to a measure to the physician. The prosecutionary authorities described the fear as unjustifiable. (Ploem et al 2021) However, also unjustifiable fear can have substantial consequences for practice.

Some empirical observations 2: palliative sedation

In the Netherlands continuous terminal sedation is allowed when there are refractory symptoms and the patient's life expectancy is less than two weeks (NHG 2022). The aim is to ease the natural death which occurs as a result of their underlying disease and does not hasten it. During continuous palliative sedation no fluids are administered. Hastening death as a result of dehydration would be a concern when the patient is sedated too early. Den Hartogh points out that the upper-limit of life expectancy should be closer to four than fourteen days if one wants to be sure palliative sedation (without fluids administered) is not life shortening. (Den Hartogh p. 122-124) So one could conclude that the upper limit in the Netherlands clearly does not exclude the possibility of hastening death, a form of slow euthanasia.

Another important empirical finding is the recently published increase of continuous palliative sedation. It increased from being used in 8% of deaths in 2005 to 12% in 2010, 18% in 2015 and most recently 23% of deaths in 2021. (Van der Heide et al 2023, p. 122) To my knowledge, there is no clear explanation for this increase in the past 20 years. Suggestions include on the one hand more familiarity with the procedure in physicians and thus more confidence that the process goes according to plan, and the hypothesis that dying patients now tolerate less suffering (than they did in the past). The most recent study of continuous palliative sedation in nursing homes in the Netherlands describes the period 2007-2011, when already 21% of the nursing home residents with severe dementia received continuous palliative sedation at the end of life, the three main refractory symptoms being pain, shortness of breath an agitation.(Hendriks et al 2014) This seems to be a relatively large percentage at that time compared to palliative sedation in the whole population (21% vs 10-12%), but of course there are also differences in the higher likelihood of certain symptoms as a result of dementia and the lower likelihood of an accidental death once admitted to a nursing home.

In addition to these data, there is an observation from the cases described by GPs(-in-training), that there appear to be regular instances of continuous sedation in patients with advanced dementia. GPs-in-training sometimes express worry about whether these cases fulfil the requirement of a (short) less than two weeks life expectancy.

Finally, there is an additional guideline with respect to palliative sedation in patients with dementia and refractory problematic behaviour (Verenso 2022). This guideline clarifies the conditions which justify continuous sedation to manage refractory problematic behaviour in patients with dementia. Problem behaviour is defined as causing suffering or danger to the patient or others. It can consist of psychotic episodes, apathy, distress, etc. In order for this behaviour to be qualified as refractory, all other methods to lessen the (suffering as a result of the) problematic behaviour (including intermittent sedation) must have been employed, and the suffering of the patient themselves must be severe. In the guideline it is stated that such refractory problematic behaviour in itself is a sign of the terminal phase, while in another part of the guideline it is clarified that the life expectancy in patients with advanced dementia is unclear because their dying process involves a longer period of "dwindling". (Verenso 2022)

Consequently the guideline states that continuous palliative sedation for refractory problem behaviour in patients with advanced dementia is indicated when the behaviour causes severe suffering in the patient and the patient's death is *reasonably* to be expected within two weeks. (Verenso 2022)

This combination of uncertainty of the length of the dying phase combined with the rather wide variety of possible problem behaviours leaves these patients with less safeguards than those patients qualifying for continuous palliative sedation as a result of suffering from refractory symptoms in the dying phase of for instance a terminal cancer. I would contend this guideline leaves room for too early palliative sedation.

Working hypothesis

In summary, there is a very limited number of cases of euthanasia performed in patients who are suffering from advanced dementia as a result – amongst other things – of fear of review and prosecution, and there is an increasing use of continuous palliative sedation. Perhaps this (also) concerns patients with advanced dementia suffering from problem behaviour, where it appears that there are less safeguards against too early continuous sedation as a consequence of the uncertainty of their life expectancy.

This leads to the hypothesis that in some cases instead of having their euthanasia request honoured on the basis of an AED, these patients are sedated, and some of them perhaps too early and thus not softening death but causing it. This clearly raises an empirical question, which need to be answered.

In this paper I take this hypothesis which is not implausible, further to consider the evident ethical questions that follow. The hypothesis fits with the point Den Hartogh argues that in the less regulated, normal, medical practice, there seems to be no (expectation of) misuse. He points out the selective fear for murderous physicians when one legalises euthanasia, while overlooking the far more frequent opportunities they have to edge those in the palliative phase towards death by other means. (Den Hartogh p. 202-203)

This issue becomes more pressing as a result of the expected increase in the number of patients suffering from dementia, some of whom are struggling, suffering or showing problematic behaviour, and some with family members advocating an end to the suffering.

Does early palliative sedation in patients with advanced dementia constitute active-ending-of-life?

I would like to revisit the question which acts constitute active ending of life. Den Hartogh argues that early sedation whilst withholding fluids is homicide. (Den Hartogh p. 124) As pointed out before, Den Hartogh is more strict than the general guideline for continuous palliative sedation in the Netherlands, and would presumably consider early sedation on the basis of dysregulated problem behaviour in a patient with (advanced) dementia active ending of life, and consequently homicide. Here I want to address whether there is any wriggle room in this conclusion.

One approach is to consider the uncertainty about life expectancy, particularly in patients with advanced dementia. It can be difficult to estimate life expectancy in general, but particularly in patients with dementia. (Verenso 2022) In a quantitative study of the last week of patients with dementia, physicians expected only 88% of the patients to die, and some of them died earlier than expected.(Hendriks 2014) Thus it might not be possible to estimate a life expectancy of no more than 2 weeks accurately. Does the level of uncertainty mean that it is better to err on the safe, definitely not the active ending of life side, in other words, to use palliative sedation only when it is abundantly clear the patient is about to die? Or can the longer period of dying be taken as a reason to be less concerned about the exact life expectancy, as one physician states in a qualitative study on dying under continuous palliative sedation:

> Well, in my opinion those two weeks are not a real critical boundary; it can be something more and something less, but it's the idea of the approaching death anyway, so that plays a role. (Veldwijk-Rouwenhorst et al 2021)

If the life expectancy is unclear and the decision to start palliative sedation is taken nevertheless, should that be viewed as (slow) active ending of life? Where should the boundary be: a life-expectancy of a week, of a few days, or only several hours? The issue with erring on the safe side without any risk or intention of life-shortening, is that this leaves some patients suffering unbearably. The same qualitative study on palliative sedation in nursing homes describes the despair caregivers and family members experience when no intervention appears to lessen the burden and suffering of the patient. (Veldwijk-Rouwenhorst et al 2021) Is *in dubio abstine* the right moral action, is openly performing active ending of life though euthanasia on the basis of an advance euthanasia directive in these patients the answer, or is a possibly early palliative sedation the right course of action?

I conclude that while there is a zone in which palliative sedation is clearly not slow active ending of life, and a zone in which it surely is (slow) active ending of life, there is also a grey zone between these and it is unlikely that this will disappear. The active ending of life or not-active ending of life dichotomy fits uneasily with the uncertainty in practice.

Another approach is to revisit the distinction between active ending of life and shortening the dying phase. In the past it was common to administer muscle relaxants to newborns that were gasping after being taken off the life support, which could hasten death a little in order to spare parents the last phase which to them looked very uncomfortable. It was argued at the time that parental interest could play a role in these cases, considering that death was unavoidable and the newborn was not harmed. (Willems et al 2014). This practice has now ceased and the approach to gasping is to inform and support parents. (Ploem et al 2022) However, one could ask whether shortening the dying phase can be considered qualitatively different from active ending of life.

I would, contend that too early continuous palliative sedation on the basis of dysregulated behaviour in a patient with dementia should be considered slow active ending of life. Some uncertainty remains and in the grey area between too early palliative sedation and palliative sedation which only provides comfort during the dying phase, there are cases where it is impossible to ascertain whether something is active ending of life or not. The moral weight and possible legal consequences of active ending of life seem too heavy in cases where there is true uncertainty, while not acknowledging the possibility of active ending also misses the point. The legal framework whereby something is or is not active ending of life is not doing justice to the complexity of the practice.

What are the risks of slow active ending of life? And to whom?

If active ending of life through early palliative sedation occurs (more than occasionally), such a practice clouds the transparency surrounding active ending of life that the Netherlands has achieved through its clear legislation for euthanasia and active ending of life in newborns. The reasoning behind the regulation of active ending of life appears to be a trade-off between protection against prosecution for those physicians willing to perform careful active ending of life and transparency. Physicians are expected to be completely open about exactly what they do. One of the cornerstones of this practice is trust in physicians, both to do what is right for their patients and to be honest and open about what they are doing. If it comes to light that there is a shadow practice of slow active ending of life, this will damage the expectation of transparency and most likely reduce trust in physicians. This could do serious damage to the active ending of life practice in the Netherlands.

Moreover, an unregulated and opaque practice of slow active ending of life in patients with advanced dementia would risk arbitrariness. On the one hand, there are concerns about unjustifiable active ending of life in those patients who do not request it, and would even object to it, if they were still competent. Besides, refractory problematic behaviour as an indication for continuous palliative sedation might in practice prove too unclear. The definition and examples given in the guideline of possible problematic behaviours is quite broad, which leaves much room for interpretation. Even though the examples described in the literature are indeed convincing about the suffering of the patients, a lack of close scrutiny combined with staff shortages and an increasing nursing home population may lead to suffering being deemed refractory at an early stage (before all other interventions have been tried) or to attribute suffering to the patient, when actually the burden is too heavy for the care personnel.

On the other hand, it is not unlikely that slow active ending of life provides a good death for some patients, allowing them to escape unbearable suffering in circumstances when access to euthanasia proper is very difficult. However, if the practice of slow active ending of life is not transparent and not quite in line with the existing guidelines, patients and their family (or other representatives) have no insights in the possible existence of slow active ending of life, and as a result have no chance to consider and discuss whether slow active ending of life would be something that would be a fitting death for them.

Slow active ending of life confronts physicians with new ethical dilemmas. What should they do for their suffering patients, should they only perform active ending of life in patients with a clear advance euthanasia directive, and restrict themselves to good palliative care in all other cases? What would the right course of action be with a patient who is clearly suffering unbearably but did not write and advance euthanasia directive? Physicians might not know where the legal boundaries are between euthanasia, homicide, slow active ending of life and palliative sedation. Moreover, in practice it is unlikely that all instances of slow active ending of life or standard palliative care can be correctly labelled afterwards.

Conclusion

In this paper I present evidence that doctors' fear and other barriers preclude access to euthanasia for patients with advanced dementia. Still, these patients suffer unbearably as a result of refractory symptoms. At the same time there is an increase in the use of continuous palliative sedation at the end of life across all deaths. This leads to the hypothesis that continuous palliative sedation is used as slow active ending of life in some of these patients. If true, this raises ethical challenges, both regarding the definition of active ending of life, with its legal consequences and moral weight, and to the current, open practice of active ending of life in the Netherlands. The discovery of a shadow practice of slow euthanasia in nursing homes is highly likely to damage both trust in physicians in general and in the euthanasia practice most Dutch people value. The reason for this is mainly related to the risks of unjustified slow active ending of life of patients with advanced dementia. More empirical work is needed to elucidate the decisions and practice of continuous palliative sedation in patients with advanced dementia, in order to assess whether the hypothesis posed here is correct and which of the ethical concerns raised are particularly pressing in practice.

About the author

Eva C. A. Asscher (e.c.asscher@amsterdamumc.nl) is assistant professor of medical ethics at the AmsterdamUMC. Her current research focuses on ethical issues at the end of life, as well as public health ethics.

Literature

Bolt, EE, Snijdewind, MC, Willems, DL, et al, "Can physicians conceive of performing euthanasia in case of psychiatric disease, dementia or being tired of living?" *Journal of Medical Ethics* 41 (2015) 592-598. doi: 10.1136/medethics-2014-102150. Epub 2015 Feb 18. PMID: 25693947.

Den Hartogh G, *What Kind of Death, The Ethics of Determining One's Own Death*. New York and London: Routledge, 2023.

Den Hartogh, G.A. "Een arrest dat om uitleg vraagt", *Rechtsgeleerd Magazijn Themis* 182 (2021) 1, 26-33. https://www.uitgeverijparis.nl/nl/reader/209169/1001530697.

Harnas S, Toersen W, "Rapport meldactie 'Wilsverklaring'", Patiëntenfederatie Nederland, 2018.

Heide A van der, Legemaate J, ONwuteaka-Philipsen B, Bosma F, van Delden H, Mevis P, Mink K, Pasman R, Postma L, Renckens S, van Thiel G, van de Vathorst S, *Vierde evaluatieWet toetsing levensbeëindiging op verzoek en hulp bij zelfdoding*. Den Haag: ZonwMW, 2023.

Hendriks, S. A, Smalbrugge M, Hertogh, C.M.P.M, Van der Steen, J.T, "Dying With Dementia: Symptoms, Treatment, and Quality of Life in the Last Week of Life", *Journal of Pain and Symptom Management*, 47 (2014) 4, 710-720 https://doi.org/10.1016/j.jpainsymman.2013.05.015.

Hertogh, C. M, de Boer, M. E, Dröes, R. M, Eefsting, J. A. "Would we rather lose our life than lose our self? Lessons from the Dutch debate on euthanasia for patients with dementia", *Am J Bioeth* 7 (2007) 4, 48-56. doi: 10.1080/15265160701220881. PMID: 17454999.

Kivipelto, M, Ngandu, T, Laatikainen, T, Winblad, B, Soininen, H, Tuomilehto, J. "Risk score for the prediction of dementia risk in 20 years among middle aged people: a longitudinal, population-based study", *Lancet Neurol*. 5 (2006) 9,735-41. doi: 10.1016/S1474-4422(06)70537-3. PMID: 16914401.

Kleijne, I, "Artsen starten petitie tegen euthanasie bij dementie", *Medisch Contact* 6-2-2017.

KNMG "KNMG Standpunt / Beslissingen rond het levenseinde 2021" https://data.maglr.com/3230/issues/27397/360234/downloads/knmg_standpunt_levenseinde_interactieve_downloadversie.pdf.

Lopez, Soria JA, González, H. M,. Léger, G. C, "Chapter 13 – Alzheimer's disease", Editor(s): Steven, T. Dekosky, Sanjay Asthana, *Handbook of Clinical Neurology*, Elsevier, Volume 167,2019, Pages 231-255, ISSN 0072-9752, ISBN 9780128047668, https://doi.org/10.1016/B978-0-12-804766-8.00013-3.

NHG, Richtlijn palliatieve sedatie 2022 https://palliaweb.nl/richtlijnen-palliatieve-zorg/richtlijn/palliatieve-sedatie.

Ott, A, Breteler, M. M. B, Birkenhäger-Gillesse, E. B, van Harskamp, F, de Koning, I, Hofman, A, "De prevalentie bij ouderen van de ziekte van Alzheimer, vasculaire dementie en dementie bij de ziekte van Parkinson; het ERGO-onderzoek", *Ned Tijdschr Geneeskd*. 140 (1996) 200-5.

Ploem, M. C, Krol, E, Asscher E. C. A, Floor, T, Woestenburg, N. O. M, van de Vathorst, S, Gevers, J. K. M, Winter, H. B, "Evaluatie; Regeling beoordelingscommissie late zwangerschapsafbreking en levensbeëindiging bij pasgeborenen", Den Haag: ZonMW, 2022.

Regeling van de Minister van Veiligheid en Justitie en de Minister van Volksgezondheid, Welzijn en Sport van 11 december 2015, kenmerk 885614-145412-PG, houdende instelling van een commissie voor de beoordeling van gemelde gevallen van late zwangerschapsafbreking en levensbeëindiging bij pasgeborenen (Regeling beoordelingscommissie late zwangerschapsafbreking en levensbeëindiging bij pasgeborenen).

Regionale Toetsingscommmissies euthanasie (RTE), Jaarverslag 2022. Utrecht 2023.

Regionale Toetsingscommissies euthanasie (RTE) Euthanasiecode 2022. Utrecht 2022.

Rozemond, N, "Een mensenrechtelijke interpretatie van de uitspraken van de Hoge Raad over euthanasie bij mensen met dementie", *Rechtsgeleerd magazijn Themis*, april 2021.

Schuurmans et al. "Euthanasia in advanced dementia; the view of the general practitioners in the Netherlands on a vignette case along the juridical and ethical dispute", *BMC Family Practice* 22 (2021) 232 https://doi.org/10.1186/s12875-021-01580-z.

Stoeldraijer, L, van Duin, C, and Huisman, C, "Statistische trends, Bevolkingsprognose 2017–2060: 18,4 miljoen inwoners in 2060", Statistische Trends CBS, 2017.

Supreme Court of The Netherlands (Hoge Raad), 21 April 2020 ECLI:NL:HR:2020:712. https://deeplink.rechtspraak.nl/uitspraak?id=ECLI:NL:HR:2020:712

Veldwijk-Rouwenhorst, A. E, Smalbrugge, M, Zuidema, S. U, Hanssen, S. A. J, Koopmans, R. T. C. M, Gerritsen, D. L, "Continuous Palliative Sedation in Nursing Home Residents With Dementia and Refractory Neuropsychiatric Symptoms", *Journal of the American Medical Directors Association* 22 (2021) 2. https://doi.org/10.1016/j.jamda.2020.11.004.

Verenso, "Palliatieve sedatie bij refractair probleemgedrag bij mensen met dementie", 2022. https://www.verenso.nl/kwaliteit/richtlijnen-en-praktijkvoering/richtlijnendatabase/palliatieve-sedatie-bij-refractair-probleemgedrag-bij-mensen-met-dementie-handreiking.

Willems, D. L, Verhagen, A. A, van Wijlick, E, "Committee End-of-Life Decisions in Severely Ill Newborns of Royal Dutch Medical Association. Infants' best interests in end-of-life care for newborns", *Pediatrics*, 134 (2014) 4, 1163-8. doi: 10.1542/peds.2014-0780. Epub 2014 Sep 22. PMID: 25246628.

Response to Comments

Govert den Hartogh

Abstract
Thanks to all commentators for their words of praise and constructive criticism. I was pleasantly surprised by the fact that so many of them address the basic argument of my book, starting from the division of labour between the principles of respect for autonomy and compassion or beneficence, and resulting in my proposal of a 'dual track' system of legal regulation. The whole argument is well summarized by both Wayne Sumner and Isra Black.[1] Together the comments provide a sustained examination of every major step in that argument. I will consider them step by step.

Keywords: suicide, self-determination, right to life, Volenti, dual track, legal certainty, sedation.

Respect for autonomy and beneficence

I was very happy when I heard from Peter Rijpkema and Gijs van Donselaar that they had found Wayne Sumner prepared to give the keynote address in the conference on my book that they were organizing, for I regard his own book on the subject (*Assisted Death* 2011) the one book in a vast literature that should be regarded obligatory reading for everyone interested in that subject. Sumner starts his comments by making some remarks about my understanding of the right to end one's own life. He quotes me as saying that the decision to exercise that right has an authority that doesn't depend on its prudential and moral quality. Sumner observes that one Hohfeldian element that this right contains is a liberty. It is true that in most countries (for the

---

1   See also Fakonti 2023; Postma 2023.

Gijs van Donselaar, Peter Rijpkema, and Henri Wijsbek (eds), *The Ethics of Determining One's Own Death. Essays on Den Hartogh's What Kind of Death.*
Taylor & Francis Group, 2025
DOI: https://doi.org/10.5117/FEP2024.1.010.HART

exceptions see page 29 of my book) suicide is not forbidden. One common reason for the recognition of this liberty is that suicide is supposedly always an irrational act, and it makes no sense to make people accountable for such acts. However, a mere liberty is not a right; a liberty only becomes a right if it is protected by the duties and, perhaps, the disabilities of others.[2] The right to determine the manner and time of one's own death, as it has been recognized by the European Court of Human Rights in *Haas* (2011), correlates to a duty of others not to interfere, and, arguably, their disability to weigh this duty against other duties. Unlike the liberty this right is restricted to rational decisions.

That restriction is often understood to be motivated by the wish to prevent the suicidal person to cause harm to herself. But on the view of the European Court the claim-right is derived from the right to self-determination. And, as Germany's Federal Constitutional Court explicitly recognized,[3] the restriction of the claim to non-interference to rational suicide is implied by this derivation itself. If a person decides to act in a certain way without having any idea of the consequences of what she is about to do, or without the ability to evaluate these consequences in terms of her own values, she is not cutting her way through the jungle of life but wandering around in the dark. That is why both the European and the German Court insist on safeguards guaranteeing that the claim to non-interference is only given to people with sufficient decisional capacities to be allowed an authority about ending their lives.

Sumner suggests, however, that in defending this restriction I am still implicitly appealing to the wish to prevent self-harm. In Chapter 3 I argued that the kind of suicide that is studied by suicidologists is characteristically executed by violent means, more or less decided upon on the spot, without communication with friends and family. These characteristics usually go together. Suicides of this kind are rightly presumed to be irrational. Usually, they are not only harmful to the suicidal person, but also to the people close to her, often extremely harmful. If, on the other hand, a suicide is non-violent, considered in dialogue with others, and performed in their presence, it will tend to be both rational and beneficial to the person who ends her life, and at least much less harmful to others. Hence the restriction on the claim to non-interference that I accept actually serves both the 'prudential and moral quality' of the decision. On my own account, therefore, the principles

---

2   Sumner 1987, 48.
3   Bundesverfassungsgericht 26/2/2020, 2BvR 2347/15, § 232ff; cf. Den Hartogh 2020.

of respect for autonomy and beneficence are not so opposed to each other as I initially suggest.[4]

Let me first note that the clustering of the 'two kinds of suicide' that I postulated is not perfect. (p. 49-50 of my book) As a consequence the decision to end one's life in a violent and lonely way can only be presumed to be irrational, the presumption is defeasible. More importantly, I don't dispute the old saying, that whatever is desired is desired under the guise of the good. That is even the case when a person who is in the grip of paranoia, decides to end his life rather than to be tortured to death by his imaginary enemies. It is also true that rational suicides tend to be less harmful than irrational ones. But if a suicide is rational, in the sense of satisfying reasonable requirements of decisional capacity, that is no guarantee at all that it is not overall harmful, either to the person herself or to others. To mention but a few of a long list of systematic defects in rational decision-making that social psychologists and behavioral economists have identified over the years: undue discounting of the future, framing effects, overestimation of future emotions including regret. People are particularly bad in reckoning with probabilities. Even if people are not very good at promoting their own good, it might still be the case that they are, on the whole, better at it, or at least more reliable in *bona fide* attempting it, than any *ex ante* identifiable others, including state officials and doctors. But even that is far from obviously true, in particular in cases in which some people have an enormous advantage in some area of relevant expertise like medicine. This may explain why according to the professional morality of doctors the consent of the client is a necessary but not a sufficient condition for diagnostic and treatment.

Interestingly, in his book, Sumner considered the case of patients who take insufficient account of alternative options to alleviate their suffering, acknowledging that this would not necessarily mean that they had insufficient decision-making capacity.[5] Think of cases in which people with some assistance might still succeed in reconciling themselves to the inevitable losses of physical and mental capacities involved in ageing. In these cases concern for the patient's well-being would require a 'mild paternalism'. But there are many other kinds of cases with a similar ratio between well-being and autonomy. To mention only one such case: many patients are, quite

---

4   In Den Hartogh 2016 I defended the view that attributing the authority to make any decision to a person depends both on her decisional capacities and on the risks involved to her and others' well-being. That argument strengthens the convergence between the two principles. But even if the area of possible conflict is reduced in this way, that still doesn't mean that it is not significant at all.
5   Sumner 2011, 91.

understandably, concerned about the burdens of care that their illness imposes on their relatives or other informal care-providers. That may be a reason for them to opt for shortening their lives, even if their relatives are quite willing and capable to provide that care, and even interpret this very choice as rebuffing their love. Such situations are a common subject of discussion between patients and their relatives, and therefore also a possible subject of disagreement between patients and doctors.

The right to self-determination and the right to life

Thomas Mertens thinks that the right to end one's own life has the status for me of an 'ethical atom'. I use the term in a quotation from Bert Keizer (p. 159), but I don't believe in ethical atoms myself; even the most basic moral belief has to be understood in the context of a larger whole of moral beliefs. The subtitle of my book, *The Ethics of Determining one's own Death*, was not meant to *proclaim* a right to determine the manner and time of one's own death, but to announce an intention to investigate the existence and extension of this right. Accordingly I first set out to argue for the view that the right to self-determination contains such a right and then went on to determine its extension in the rest of the book. As Sumner observes, my view of that extension is at least in one respect more limited than the common beliefs in liberal states such as the Netherlands and Canada: on my view the right doesn't contain a power to authorize another person to end one's life. As Jurriaan de Haan recalls, from my first papers on euthanasia on I have criticized the view, dominant at the time in Dutch health law and in particular in the pioneering work of Henk Leenen, that the right to self-determination was a kind of super-right underlying all other negative rights, including the right to life. On my view the right to self-determination is just one basic right among others, including the right to personal freedom, to bodily integrity, to freedom of thought, conscience and religion, and so on.

On a view like Leenen's the right to life is essentially the power to make decisions about the extent of other people's claims and obligations as regards one's life. If the right, however, is unwaivable, such a choice-theory of the right is much less attractive. The most natural view of the right anyway is to consider it to protect the rightholder's normal interest in life, hence to hold an interest-theory of the right. One of the standard objections to this theory is that all people have an equal right to life, while their interests in continued living are very variable in weight. The first draft of my book contained a chapter on the interest-theory of the right to life that I later replaced by a summary. In that chapter[6] I tried to answer this first objection by analyzing what it means for a right to 'protect' an interest. The right does so, I suggested, by disempowering other people to determine the moral weight of the interest. That is why equal rights protect unequal interests. Only in some clearly delineated cases the protection is canceled, because some other interest evidently outweighs the interest in life. One such exception to the prohibition of killing is universally accepted: doctors are allowed to use drugs with a life-shortening side-effect when this is the only way to alleviate a dying person's severe suffering. Permitting euthanasia is a second exception of that kind. It is fully compatible with an interest-theory of the right to life and does not require us to deny that the right is unwaivable.

As Mertens observes, I am reluctant to say that my life is my property, but the reason is not the one he suggests. That people have the right to own property is a basic right, but actual property rights are legally restricted in all kinds of ways. For example, in the Netherlands the expropriation of land for building dykes has always been a legal option, and the construction of railways since 1840 made it urgent to codify these rules.[7] It has even been claimed that having a property right to something only means that you have those rights left to the use of that something that have not explicitly been taken away from you by the law. In contrast the right to self-determination, although equally open to legal specification at its periphery, has a much more robust core to which, I argued, the right to end one's life belongs. I have no qualms about accepting the existence of duties to one-self, and I also agree that some suicides violate such a duty. (p. 166) But duties to oneself, however real, are not enforceable. All things considered, my sovereignty over my personal domain, is much more sturdy than a mere property-right. But that doesn't mean that it is unlimited.

Mertens contends that the view he ascribes to me is in conflict with Art. 2 of the European Convention of Human Rights, as understood by the European Court of Human Rights. To which law, then, do I appeal for my view, he asks, perhaps to a natural law? I believe that so-called 'moral rights' that have not been conventionally or legally recognized are mere 'manifesto rights', as Joel Feinberg called them, moral considerations in search of proper recognition.[8] Such manifesto rights don't satisfy an essential condition for rights having their characteristic normative, including moral force: that the actions implementing the right are the object of the legitimate expectations

---

6   Presently under consideration for separate publication.
7   See https://ilibrariana.wordpress.com/2012/02/01/het-crommel-spoorlijntje-van-crommelin/
8   Feinberg 1973, p. 63-64.

of others. We can hold each other accountable for violating them. But these expectations can only be legitimate ones if they withstand moral criticism. Rights, therefore, have a Janus-face: they are social facts with a normative effect. If the relevant social fact did not exist, it could not have its special normative effects either, but it doesn't have those effects automatically. Correspondingly, rights claims can be defective in two different ways: the rights appealed to can fail to be socially recognized in the proper way, embedded in a pattern of mutual expectations, and they can fail to make good on the moral claim they imply. That view doesn't commit me to a belief in natural laws.[9] In addition legal claims about rights can be open to conceptual criticism.

As a matter of fact it is on both moral and conceptual grounds that I criticized the statement of the European Court in the Pretty-case that the right to life "is unconcerned with issues to do with the quality of living or what a person chooses to do with his or her life". (p. 159) This statement seems to show that the European Court subscribes neither to a choice- nor to an interest-theory of the right to life, hence presumably to the view that the right is meant to protect the impersonal value or 'dignity' of the human being. I disagree because rights are assets, not burdens.[10] My disagreement, however, doesn't derive from a belief that the right to self-determination is more fundamental than the right to life.

The limited validity of *Volenti*

If I had understood the right to self-determination to be a super-right, it would indeed, as Mertens objects, have been inconsistent for me to defend a limited form of indirect paternalism, rejecting the unrestricted applicability of *Volenti*. But if the right to life basically protects our normal interest in life and is no less fundamental than the right to self-determination, and if it is quite possible for people's decisions to be made with sufficient decision capacity and to contravene the decider's personal interests at the same time, we have to face the possibility of conflicts between both rights, and this is the context of my argument about the difference between direct and indirect paternalism.

---

9   Sumner 1987, chapter 5.
10   "Normative advantages", Sumner 1987, p. 32. Nevertheless, people might have enforceable duties to promote or respect the impersonal value of human life, see below. A human rights court is naturally tempted to redescribe such considerations as matters of 'rights'.

The argument consists of three layers. (a) I point out that there is (to my knowledge) no legal system that accepts consent as a defense in a case of homicide,[11] and I submit that such universal elements of law should be considered part of the 'considered judgments of ethical experts' that an ethical argument should attempt to accommodate. (b) I recall that the professional morality of physicians in many countries on the one hand considers the consent of the patient as a necessary but not a sufficient condition for any kind of treatment. By treating a competent person against her will, the doctor would not only violate her right to self-determination, but normally also her right to bodily integrity. On the other hand, 'first do no harm' has always been one basic element of the morality of doctors, a maxim that is all the more important because of the insurmountable asymmetry in knowledge about the possibilities of harming between the medical expert and the layperson. This consideration applies to the right to bodily integrity but it would be odd to consider consent merely necessary for medical treatment, but sufficient for medical killing. (c) Most basically, the basic moral objections to direct paternalism don't apply to the indirect variety. Having the freedom to make one's own self-regarding choices is a benefit by itself, but that particular benefit is not at stake when others are not providing assistance or are even prohibited to provide it. And the direct paternalist violates the equality of moral status ('dignity') between benefactor and beneficiary, but the indirect paternalist doesn't.[12]

To refute my first claim, the one about the universal legal element, Mertens appeals to the recent ruling by the German Constitutional Court that made legal space for suicide assistance by doctors, even by suicide assistance services. But an interesting aspect of that ruling is that the Court didn't appeal to *Volenti*. Instead it argued that the right to determine the manner and time of one's own death would be, to use the terminology of the European Court, theoretical and illusory if medical assistance in effectuating one's decision would not be available. On the one hand that claim is too strong, because even in that case almost everyone would still have the option of ending her own life by voluntarily stopping eating and drinking, if medical supervision and, if necessary, palliative care, would be

---

11 Although the presence of consent may be relevant for the identification of the proper subclass of homicide, as it is in Dutch law.
12 In his fine review of my book Paul Schotsmans calls my discussion on human dignity (p. 160-163) "very weak". What I should, indeed, have stressed more is that claims about human dignity, understood as a status, not as a value, are relevant in one other way: they underline the equality of moral status.

assured. On the other hand the argument fails to distinguish between two ways in which the doctor could provide assistance.¹³

Two kinds of assisted suicide

The upshot of my argument about the two principles is that you have a right to determine the manner and time of your own death, that is derived from your right to self-determination, but that the appeal to this right is insufficient to make it permissible for others, in particular physicians (and perhaps nurse practitioners) to assist you in ending your life in a way that makes them co-responsible for that outcome. They can only claim the right to act in that way if they can reasonably be assured that by doing so they are providing a benefit to you.

In my book, however, I argue, that this doesn't mean that no kind of what is usually called 'assistance' can be provided by anyone who is not sure enough of benefitting you. Leaving aside the position of relatives, I argue that your right to end your life implies a right to get access to the means of doing so in a humane way, for example barbiturates. My argument was that providing that access is not really a kind of 'assistance', it is only lifting a blockade.

Isra Black objects that lifting a blockade can be a kind of assistance. If my pharmacist leaves the door of his shop unclosed during the night in order to enable me to sneak in and pick up a dosage of barbiturates, he is surely assisting me in ending my life. In answering the objection I could try to be more precise about the cases in which lifting a blockade is or isn't a kind of assistance; they obviously have to do with the reasons for launching and maintaining a blockade to begin with. But the basic point is that, even if lifting a blockade is properly called a kind of assistance, we can request the blockade to be lifted in all cases in which the reasons for launching it clearly do not apply, and in that case the person who accedes to the request cannot be held responsible for any harmful effects befalling us.

But Black's second objection is that a company that produces and sells barbiturates to people who want to end their lives in a humane way, is providing a service and not merely lifting a blockade.¹⁴ That is surely correct. How damaging is that objection to my argument?

---

13 Den Hartogh 2020. The German Court seems mainly concerned with providing access to lethal drugs.
14 By now barbiturates are largely out of use because of their undesirable side-effects. In Denmark their use is already no longer allowed for any medical aim.

RESPONSE TO COMMENTS

Hemlock is a very poisonous plant, consumption of only one leaf is lethal. Actually, dying that way is not painless, you will suffer from nausea and abdominal pain. But suppose that it was painless. Suppose further that hemlock only grew in one place and that the government, in order to prevent its use for murder and suicide, had closed access to that place. In that case a person who has voluntarily and competently decided to end her own life could require the gate to be opened for her by appeal to her right of self-determination recognized in Art. 8 of the European Convention. If the gate-keeper opened the gate to her, my claim would be that this would only be a case of lifting a blockade, in a case in which the reasons for the blockade do not apply, and as such would not make the gate-keeper responsible for any harm that would befall me as a result.

This is, I submit, one end of a continuum, at the other end of which we find standard euthanasia cases as we know them from the Netherlands, Canada and a few other countries. The mistake that I made in my book, and that is identified by Black's objection, was not to recognize this continuum, but to suggest a clear dichotomy in its place.

All along the continuum there is someone involved besides the person who wants to end his life. The succeeding positions on the continuum differ from each other in the amount of *agential involvement*, as Black following Ralph Wedgwood, calls it. The question now becomes at which point on the continuum we ascribe full responsibility to that second person for causally contributing to the achievement of that end. That is important because on my argument that would mean that that second person cannot justify his involvement by merely appealing to the first person's right to self-determination plus *Volenti*. He has to show that he could reasonably believe to provide a benefit.

My first claim is that the company that produces and sells barbiturates is still fairly close to the hemlock-case, even if it does not merely lift a blockade, but provides a service. Similarly, a doctor who provides palliative care to a patient who has decided not to accept life-prolonging treatment or to stop eating and drinking in some way facilitates the execution of that decision, but that doesn't make him accountable for the death of that patient. (p. 68-69)

My second claim is the one I made in my book, that full-blown physician-assistance as it is permitted in Dutch and Canadian law is at the other end of the continuum; it is morally indistinguishable from euthanasia, a case of joint action in which both participants make essential but complementary contributions to achieving a shared aim. To use terms from the penal law, such doctors are co-participants, not mere accomplices or accessories.

Black agrees with me that the two services (providing access to lethal drugs and participation in the joint action of ending someone's life) have different degrees of agential involvement and that this justifies holding doctors accountable to different degrees for the results of patients' decisions. He goes on to argue that, even if we consider the right of access to lethal drugs as being implied by the right to self-determination, other basic values can be involved in the specification of the right. I fully agree: as he points out, I have myself referred to considerations of dignity and the importance of family relations in this respect. Preventing harm to others is of course always a relevant consideration, perhaps even including indirect harm, harm resulting from harm to self because of other people's interest in that self.[15]

What about harm to self? Black suggests that the law could forbid giving people access to medication that brings about death in a non-humane way. (Hemlock!) That is at present a quite topical issue in the Netherlands because of the activities of the Cooperation Last Will. Until the Public Prosecutor intervened the Cooperation was organizing a system that would have made sodium-azide generally available to its members. (p. 215, footnote 57) It has now been established that in a substantial number of cases the death caused by this drug is a painful one, possibly involving vomiting, epileptic fits and shortness of breath. I am inclined to agree that this could be a reason to block access, even to people who have made a voluntary and well-considered decision to use it. The justification for a prohibition might be a combination of harm to bystanders and harm to self, and it would be much stronger if access to humane means was available. In that case, however, the presumption of an irrational choice would also be very strong. Hence we would not need the appeal to self-harming to justify the prohibition.

Nevertheless, I am prepared to consider any argument for a form of 'mild paternalism' on its merits. I happen to believe that Feinberg's valiant attempts to deny the defensibility of (hard) paternalism in all cases have not been completely successful.[16] However, such an argument cannot imply that we are only justified in respecting a person's right to end her own life if we are sure that it will be in her best interests to exercise that right. The content-independent authority that the right implies may be limited in all kinds of ways, perhaps even by paternalist concerns, but it necessarily covers a significant area of prudential and moral considerations. Exercising the right

15 Sumner also raises this important issue in passing. As a matter of fact no existing regulatory system for assisted death takes this kind of indirect harm to others into account, but perhaps this is a defect of such systems. It may be one of the reasons why most doctors are reluctant to end a person's life when her relatives oppose her decision. Cf. Feinberg 1984, pp. 70-79, distinguishing between other-regarding or vicarious and indirectly self-regarding interests.

16 Arneson 2005; cf. Den Hartogh 2016 on the fluidity of the borderline between soft and hard paternalism.

will therefore inevitably sometimes have unfortunate consequences from a prudential and even from a moral point of view. Moreover, the authority itself is derived from the value of self-determination alone, even if possible *limitations* to the authority are derived from other considerations.

The dual track approach: deeply perplexing?

Sumner nicely summarizes my argument about the 'hard classes': the elderly, suffering from an accumulation of old-age ailments or other negative effects of aging (loneliness), people suffering primarily from a mental illness, and persons in the early stages of dementia. For these groups, I argue, it is much more difficult for doctors to be sure that, in accepting a request for euthanasia, they are really benefitting those persons. But even people from these groups retain the right to determine the manner and time of their own death and therefore the right to have access to humane means, provided only that they make that decision in a voluntary, well-considered and stable way.

Sumner observes that the Canadian law addresses the special problem posed by the hard cases in another way: by adding additional procedural safeguards, without deleting any of the existing ones.[17] In his eyes my proposal is "deeply perplexing", because it makes the self-chosen death more readily available to the people who are least certain to benefit from it. His concerns are shared by Esther Pans.

But what exactly is the difference between the Canadian system and my proposal? I have no objection at all to making additional procedural requirements for establishing the voluntary, well-considered and durable character of the choice for death, requirements about waiting periods, mandatory consultation and full information. Indeed, the case for making such requirements seems very strong to me. I already registered my dissatisfaction with the legal reforms proposed by the Cooperation Last Will. The need for additional requirements is underlined by Van Wijngaarden's findings referred to by Pans, about the ambiguity and changeability of the death wishes of people who don't consider themselves to have a serious illness. On the other hand, as I will discuss in the next section, it is questionable to what extent the 'substantial requirements' about the condition of the

---

17 In Belgium a two-track system of this kind has already been introduced by the law of 2002, although with a mandatory waiting period of only one month. The Dutch EuthanasiaCode 2022 requires the consultation of at least one psychiatrist in cases concerning psychiatric disorders.

patient still have any real bite at present and will retain it in the foreseeable future. Finally, the comparison between Medical Assistance in death-laws in Canada or in the Benelux on the one hand, and in permissive American states on the other, seems to show that it is much easier for people to leave the responsibility for ending their lives to a person in a white coat than to take that responsibility themselves. In the American states the only task of the doctor is to check the voluntariness of the request and the decisional capacity of the requester. But the number of MAID-deaths in Oregon is only one sixth of the number in the Netherlands. (p. 326-327)[18] For these reasons I doubt whether the risks of self-harming involved in the system I propose really are any greater. None of the risks that Pans claims to be involved in all de-medicalized systems seems to have materialized in Oregon.

The basic question, however, is about the very distribution of responsibilities itself. If people have the right to make self-regarding decisions – even this most basic self-regarding decision of all: to be or not to be – the state doesn't have a special duty of care to make sure that the decision by itself is a beneficial one.[19] But doctors and nurses have such a duty as regards their own actions. Or so I claim.

Reinterpreting the existing law?

If I understand Jurriaan de Haan correctly, he doesn't put into question that the Dutch euthanasia law, as it passed parliament in 2001, was supposed to be justified by the doctor's duty of beneficence or mercy and the patient's right to self-determination, somehow operating in tandem. But on his view this is only a historical fact. Since then, the principle of respect for autonomy has become much more prominent, both in the application of the law and in the public debate.[20] According to De Haan that doesn't necessarily mean, however, that the law has either to be amended or to be supplemented, for

---

18 Pullman 2023 prefers the Californian MAID-law to the Canadian one because of the much lower number of MAID-deaths in California, without even noting this major difference between the systems.

19 That would also be my response to the similar concerns raised by Els van Wijngaarden in her review. This doesn't mean that I reject all paternalistic proposals out of hand. It doesn't seem a good idea to make opioids available on request.

20 As both Pans and Weyers point out, the legislator of 2001 intentionally used open norms, in order to enable social developments to shape their interpretation, see also Pans 2006, p. 367; Weyers 2023, p. 23; Legemaate, van der Heide, Mevis 2023. I don't deny this, but I doubt whether this flexibility extends to the justificatory principles of the law.

the requirements of due care can be understood to be justified by other considerations than those of the doctor's duty of care.

That the law originally implemented what De Haan calls the Joint View, can, as he observes, partly be explained by the fact that it only aimed to codify an already existing legal situation that had been created by the Supreme Court's landmark decision in the Schoonheim case (1984). That decision, on its turn, had been highly influenced by a position statement of the Board of the Royal Dutch Medical Association KNMG, that already contained the extant requirements of due care in a recognizable form.[21] Even though during the eighties and nineties the Pure autonomy view was already dominant in the public debate, representatives of the KNMG have always held on to the Joint View,[22] and in designing the law it was a priority for the government to be seen in close alliance with the profession. It was also a priority to appeal to a broader constituency than the liberal parties, including the progressive part of the Dutch churches.[23]

Is it true that the law as it stands, can, without amendment or supplementation, be justified, by the Pure view? De Haan offers two suggestions. The first is an appeal to the impersonal value of biological human life as such, similar to the view I ascribed to the European Court, as expressed in *Pretty*. Long ago, in 1886, a view of that kind had already been appealed to for justifying the criminalization of 'killing on request' in Art. 293 of the Dutch Penal Code. As the Minister of Justice Modderman then expressed the point: if there is consent, attack on the person disappears, lack of the respect that is due to human life as such remains. That statement had been quoted by the Supreme Court in *Schoonheim* (1984), and in *Brongersma* (2002) the court still distinguished between the value of life for the community and the individual. In the parliamentary debates about the euthanasia law, the government, however, did not subscribe to an interpretation of that kind of the right to life at all, but rather to an interest theory.[24] In any case, it is hard to see how the idea of the impersonal value of human life can be represented by the requirement of unrelievable and intolerable suffering.[25] It is of course not a Pure View.

---

21 Weyers 2004, ch. 6.
22 One prominent example is Dillman 1998, who appealed to the argument on *Volenti* in my paper from 1996.
23 Theologians have been prominent in advocating the legalization of euthanasia since 1970, in particular H.M. Kuitert, who defended a Joint View, but gave the authority to decide about the existence of unbearable suffering to the patient.
24 See Pans 2006, p. 147-148, 196 for relevant quotations.
25 De Haan 2000, p. 207, suggested that extreme suffering reduces the impersonal value of a person's life. That is not in accordance with the European Court's view in *Pretty*.

It is more plausible to understand the general prohibition of both killing on request and suicide assistance as being justified solely by safety concerns. Could we – this is De Haan's second suggestion – think of the 'substantial' requirements of due care in a similar way?[26] It is true that the substantial and the procedural requirements are not fully unconnected. If a patient is not informed about alternative ways of alleviating her suffering or doesn't give these options an intelligible weight in terms of her own values, that may be a reason for doubting her decisional capacity, and if she doesn't seem to be suffering at all, her very request may be hard to understand. But these are defeasible considerations that are already standardly taken into account when the voluntary, well-considered and stable character of a request is assessed. By turning them into separate requirements of due care one would, it seems, overshoot the mark. Anyone who wanted to defend that position would face a heavy burden of proof.

But, both De Haan and Pans suggest, since 2002 respect for autonomy has been given an increasingly important role in the interpretation of the requirement of unrelievable and unbearable suffering itself. I didn't find the evidence adduced for this contention in the Fourth National Survey (2023) as convincing as they do. Rather, I believe, there have been conflicting tendencies of interpretation of the law from the start.[27] For example, the Survey points to the claim made by the EuthanasiaCode 2022 that it is a subjective matter whether a patient is suffering unbearably. "This depends on the individual patient's perception of their situation, their life history and medical history, personality, values and physical and mental stamina." But the Review Committees have stated from their first Annual Report (1998) on that 'unbearable suffering' was a subjective notion, meaning that unbearability could only be established by the patient because he has exclusive access to his own mind. When the quoted sentence from the Code, on my suggestion, was first adopted in the Annual Report 2002, the point was precisely that a patient, assessing his condition in terms of his own values, could possibly be mistaken, and his assessment, therefore, open to discussion, with his relatives and his doctor, even when they looked at the situation, as they should, from his perspective.[28]

Nevertheless, I don't dispute that the committees tend to take the assessment of the patient's condition by doctor and the consultant for granted,

---

26 Suggested by the Belgian Court of Arbitration (*Arbitragehof*) 14/1/2004, B3.3.
27 As Van Delden 2003 already observed.
28 The Report 2002 therefore didn't call 'unbearable' a subjective, but a 'personalized' ('persoonsgebonden') notion. I don't know to what extent committee members these days appreciate the point.

if they concur, and even to give the doctor the benefit of the doubt, if they don't. (pp. 239-242) Heleen Weyers refers to statements made to that effect by the researchers of the Fourth Survey. But, as Weyers also emphasizes, doctors and consultants still go on to give some substance to the condition of unbearable suffering by requiring that the unbearability should at least be 'palpable' ('invoelbaar') to them.[29] In the Netherlands this may be the last defense line against an interpretation of the substantial requirements about the patient's condition that leaves it fully to him to decide whether or not they have been met. Elsewhere, in Canada, Australia and New Zealand, this is an interpretation that is already to some extent enshrined in the language of the law.

There is something troublesome about the idea of services that are only available to people who satisfy certain criteria, but who are held to satisfy them when they say so. Such requirements invite dissimulation. A notorious example was the old Dutch law that allowed married people to divorce when one of them confessed to adultery ('the great lie'). Another example is the present Dutch abortion law that only allows abortion when this is required by the woman's dire predicament ('de nood van de vrouw') and leaves it to her to decide whether her predicament is dire. If one really believes that euthanasia can be justified by the principle of respect for autonomy on its own, one should honestly advocate deleting the requirements about the patient's condition altogether. Even if one believes with De Haan that they are required for other reasons than beneficence, one should be as reluctant as I am to accept an interpretation which authorizes the patient to decide on them.

The implication of this interpretation is to make the right to life *de facto* a waivable right. That would, as I suggested already, be very odd when the right to bodily integrity in its core would still remain unwaivable.[30] If one wants to go that way, one should, therefore, also delete the requirement from medical law that the doctor should always act in accordance with 'the professional standard', hence in the patient's best interests. The patient's consent would be enough.

One advantage of the dual track approach would be that it would stop this eroding development, and thereby help to preserve the moral integrity of the euthanasia law, as well as of medical law generally. Doctors could

---

29 That is, unfortunately, also a subjective notion. Empathy is not equally distributed among doctors.
30 The right is only partly unwaivable: you can permit your barber to cut your hair, but not your doctor to amputate your leg without medical necessity. (p. 156, 168)

resist pressure by a patient by pointing to his own options and his own responsibility.[31] I can understand why De Haan calls my proposal 'extreme', recalling Sumner's perplexity. But in this respect my proposal should rather be called conservative, it aims to prevent the erosion of the existing law while proposing for the additional law requirements that are more effective in promoting safety than a fully eroded law would be.

Legal certainty: a neglected issue

Heleen Weyers points out that it was one of the major aims of the Dutch euthanasia law to promote legal certainty for physicians pondering a patient's request. The four evaluations of the law that have been performed since then conclude that this aim has been achieved, but, as Weyers shows, on less than fully convincing grounds. In particular we don't at present know what knowledge doctors generally have about the legal requirements of due care in so-called complex cases, cases involving the 'hard classes', nor – what is something different – what knowledge they have, using the EuthanasiaCode, the advice of SCEN-consultants, and other reliable sources, when they make final decisions about requests in such cases. We have information about their general knowledge from research in 2007 and 2011, showing lacunas as regards the complex cases, but at that time such cases hardly occurred at all.

We also don't know how sure doctors feel, and correctly feel, when predicting the judgments of the Review Committees. According to the president of the Committees in almost all of the few cases (13 in 2022) in which the doctor has been judged not to have satisfied the requirements, she could have easily prevented that judgment by consulting the EuthanasiaCode.[32] Probably the doctors involved relied on their own estimation without checking it. But what we in particular would like to be better informed about is the extent to which doctors refuse requests that would have been judged to conform to the requirements, because they are not sure enough that these requests *do* conform. I will discuss one category of such refusals in the next section. In addition there are clear signs that physicians, even from the Expertise Centre Euthanasia, still sometimes believe that the suffering of a very old patient has no 'medical foundation', if her ailments are not 'severe' enough.[33]

---

31 As they already can by providing information about stopping eating and drinking. On the occurrence of such pressure see p. 227-228. The Fourth Survey reports similar data.
32 Jaarverslag Regionale Toetsingscommissies Euthanasie 2022, Voorwoord.
33 Den Hartogh 2021.

I agree with Weyers that we need to know more about these matters. What we do know, however, is that the percentage of cases in which doctors grant the patient's request for euthanasia increased from 37 in 2005 to 67 in 2021, and the percentage of cases in which they refused the request because it supposedly did not meet the requirements declined more or less accordingly. (p. 226) It is difficult to evaluate this development, but I am inclined to believe that we may be moving into the direction of a system in which euthanasia is available on request. For the reasons that I have indicated I find that at least as problematic as a limited number of improper refusals.

What could we do to reduce remaining unfounded fears? The Belgian Constitutional Court has recently ordered the government to modify the euthanasia law in such a way that a physician who has failed to satisfy the legal requirements will no longer automatically be guilty of 'murder by poisoning',[34] and the Fourth Survey has recommended to consider a similar change in Dutch law.[35] But the Belgian law specifies minimum penalties for such offenses, although the courts have ways to pass by their obligations in this respect.[36] In the Netherlands, on the contrary, in the only case brought to court since 2002, doctor Arends was accused of killing by request, subsidiary of murder, but the Public Prosecutor did not request any penalty to be imposed. Disciplinary law seems therefore more threatening to Dutch physicians than criminal law. (But we don't know whether this is also their own view.)

All in all, promoting clear and correct information seems much more important to me. And preventing disinformation, in particular in medical guidelines.

Sedation until death as slow euthanasia

In the Netherlands the most controversial issue about euthanasia has been the possibility of ending the life of a person in a progressive stage of dementia on the basis of an advance directive, in particular when that patient, even if lacking decisional capacity, makes utterances suggesting a will to live. Unfortunately, the decision of the Supreme Court in the Arends-case (2020)

---

34 Grondwettelijk Hof, Arrest nr. 134/2022.
35 Van der Heide et al. 2023, 280; cf. Legemaate, Mevis, van der Heide 2023.
36 That may partly explain why the Federal Control and Evaluation Committee Euthanasia with only one exception always has found the physician to satisfy the requirements, even when she deviated from them in such obvious and significant ways as in the case of Tine Nys, cf. De Hert et al. 2022.

has not, as one could have hoped for, ended the controversy.[37] Eva Asscher suggests that, as a result, some doctors, for fear of prosecution, turn to the alternative of palliative sedation (without artificial hydration), even in cases in which it is highly uncertain, or even improbable, that the patient has such a short life-expectancy that he will not die as a result of dehydration. I would add that many doctors would prefer that alternative anyway, even if they were not afraid of the law, because they (falsely) believe that, by following this procedure, they do not kill the patient. (p. 124-130) As Asscher recognizes, they also occasionally follow it, if there is no advance directive justifying euthanasia.

I agree with Asscher that there are signs of this kind of displacement of euthanasia by palliative sedation,[38] and I also agree that we need more research to test her hypothesis. The guideline to which she refers (Verenso 2022) is highly disquieting indeed. I also agree with her that, even though a hastened death in many of these cases may be a benefit to the patients involved, in some cases it may not be, and in other cases euthanasia would have been preferable. We should therefore start discussing whether we should not introduce, preferably by professional regulation but if necessary by law, some additional requirements of due care for decisions to start deep sedation until death, at least in all cases in which the life-expectancy of the patient exceeds a few days. I am thinking, in particular, of a requirement of independent consultation.[39]

And finally...

Finally, it is a pleasure to thank Peter Rijpkema and Gijs van Donselaar for taking the initiative for the conference on my book, Peter in particular for organizing it, Henri Wijsbek and Gijs for editing this volume, and Henri, in particular, for giving detailed comments on all contributions, including my own. I consider myself lucky with such friends.

---

37   Partly because the verdict uses legalese that requires close reading to be correctly understood, partly because the EuthanasiaCode fails to properly translate this language, and partly because medical guidelines continue to make statements that conflict with the verdict. For a glaring example see Stichting Kwaliteitsimpuls Langdurige Zorg, *Handreiking Beslisvaardigheid en Wilsbekwaamheid* 2024, 33-34.
38   For example public statements by doctors who criticized doctor Arends, suggesting that they would have opted for palliative sedation in her case.
39   As I already pleaded for in my comment on the first edition of the KNMG-guideline Palliative Sedation, Den Hartogh 2006.

RESPONSE TO COMMENTS

About the author

Govert den Hartogh (g.a.denhartogh@uva.nl) is Emeritus Professor of Moral Philosophy at the University of Amsterdam, The Netherlands.

Literature

Arneson, R. J."Joel Feinberg and the justification of hard paternalism", *Legal Theory* 11 (2005) 3, 259–284.
Delden, H van, "Het juiste moment voor euthanasie", in: M. Adams, J. Griffiths, G. den Hartogh (red) *Euthanasie: Nieuwe Knelpunten in een Voortgezette Discussie*, Kampen: Kok, 2003.
Dillman, R. "Euthanasie: de morele grondslag van de arts", in: J. Legemaate, R. Dillman (red.) *Levensbeëindigend handelen door de arts op verzoek van de patiënt*, Houten: Bohn Stafleu van Loghum, 1998.
Fakonti, C. "Book Review of Govert den Hartogh, *What Kind of Death*", *Medical Law Review*, 31 (2023) 416.
Feinberg, J. *Social Philosophy*. Englewood Cliffs, NJ: Prentice Hall, 1973.
Feinberg, J. *Harm to Others*. Oxford: Oxford UP, 1984.
Haan, J. de, *The Possibility of Moral Dilemmas*. Doctoral dissertation, 2000.
Hartogh, G. A. den, "Palliatieve sedatie en euthanasie: commentaar op een richtlijn", *Tijdschrift voor Gezondheidsrecht* 30 (2006) 2, 109–119.
Hartogh, G. A. den, "Do we need a threshold conception of competence?", *Medicine, Health Care and Philosophy* 19 (2016) 71–83.
Hartogh, G. A. den, "Decriminalizing assisted suicide services: a comment on the decision of the German Federal Constitutional Court (Bundesverfassungsgericht) of 26 February 2020", *European Constitutional Law Review* 16 (2020) 713–732.
Hartogh, G. A. den, "'Voltooid leven' en de grenzen van het medisch domein", *Tijdschrift voor Gezondheidsrecht* 45 (2021) 1, 5-14.
Heide, A. van der et al. *Vierde evaluatie. Wet toetsing levensbeëindiging op verzoek en hulp bij zelfdoding*, Den Haag: ZonMw, 2023.
Hert, M. et al. "Improving control over euthanasia of persons with psychiatric illness", *Frontiers in Psychiatry* 13 (2022) 933748.
Legemaate, J, Mevis, P. Van der Heide, A. "Vijftig jaar euthanasie(beleid)", *Nederlands Juristenblad* 40 (2023) 3466-3476.
Pans, E. *De Normatieve Grondslagen van het Nederlandse Euthanasierecht*. Tilburg: Wolf Legal Publishing, 2006.
Postma, L. "Boekbespreking Govert den Hartogh, *What Kind of Death*", *Tijdschrift voor Gezondheidsrecht*, 33 (2023) 5, 488.

Pullman, D. "Slowing the slide down the slippery slope of Medical Assistance in Dying", *American Journal of Bioethics* 23 (2023) 11, 64-72.

Schotsmans, P. "Review of Govert den Hartogh, *What Kind of Death*", *European Journal of Health Law* 30 (2023) 5, 603-607.

Sumner, L. W. *The Moral Foundations of Rights*. Oxford: Clarendon Press, 1987.

Sumner, L. W. *Assisted Death: A Study in Ethics and Law*. Oxford: Oxford U.P. 2011.

Weyers, H. *Euthanasie: het proces van rechtsverandering*. Amsterdam: Amsterdam UP, 2004.

Weyers, H. *Euthanasie in Nederland 2002-2022*. Den Haag: Boom juridisch, 2023.

Wijngaarden, E. van. "Boekbespreking: de Ethiek van het Zelfgekozen Levenseinde", *Tijdschrift voor Gezondheidszorg en Ethiek* 33, 2023.

This Kind of Death? The Practice of Self-Euthanasia Illustrated

Ton Vink

Abstract

As Den Hartogh makes it known in the opening-paragraph of his Introduction to *What kind of Death*: "By now much is known about the preferences people have regarding the manner and time of their own death." In this paper I will illustrate the actual practice of one of those preferences: self-euthanasia. I define self-euthanasia as 'the deliberate termination of his or her own life by the person himself, under his own control, after clear and careful consideration, and carried out with due care'. After indicating in a few lines what makes this kind of death a *good* death, I will say goodbye to *theory* and illustrate the *practice* of this kind of death by three of the many cases of self-euthanasia that I have been involved in during my days as counselor. In two of the cases presented here, I was present when the self-euthanasia was effected.

Keywords: self-euthanasia, euthanasia, good death.

Introductory: self-*eu*thanasia

First, in a few lines: what allows us to refer to a certain kind of death as a *good* death? The fact that we as humans die, should come as no surprise. Our mortality is part of our being human. We may regret that eventually we all have to die, but that, in a way, means regretting we are humans. There are, however, several kinds of *good* death, several ways to die a *good* death, one of them being self-euthanasia[1].

---

[1] Elsewhere I have also discussed the other, better known variety of 'euthanasia', in which the physician plays a vital and decisive part and to which I therefore refer as 'physician-euthanasia'.

Gijs van Donselaar, Peter Rijpkema, and Henri Wijsbek (eds), *The Ethics of Determining One's Own Death. Essays on Den Hartogh's What Kind of Death.*
Taylor & Francis Group, 2025
DOI: https://doi.org/10.5117/FEP2024.1.011.VINK

The following are the constituent parts of this particular good death:
(a) death is decidedly self-chosen after clear and careful consideration
(b) in it, the individual's role is as large as possible
(c) it is carried out with the utmost care, without pain or suffering added
(d) death is not executed in forced loneliness
(e) if at all possible, prepared in contact with loved ones
(f) considered (given the circumstances) as dignified
(g) and accepted by the individual in peace and quiet.

Two further constituent parts, vital in the case of self-euthanasia, are:
(h) death is self-performed, and
(i) death is self-determined.

Constituent parts (h) and (i), and also (b), are the ones that most clearly mark the difference between physician-euthanasia and self-euthanasia.

A Room with a View, the case of Anton

And what a view! A magnificent and undisturbed panoramic view over the Lower Rhine near Arnhem, life on and around the river. Not the worst view for a biologist and the binoculars in his room were there for a reason. Although I had not been invited by Anton in early October 2011 because of the view, there was no escaping it, because of the location of the apartment building and the layout of the rooms.

A thorough conversation
Anton – we shared our first name, though in my case the inspiration rested clearly with St. Anthony – had turned 86 that year. And, all things considered, he had had enough. I report on his farewell of life with his permission, but without his last name.

Anton had learned to live with the increasing limitations of his physical abilities over the years, until the crucial limit had now been reached in his eyes. His decision that he would not live through that year's Christmas and New Year's Eve was settled as far as he was concerned. And settled by

---

For this part of 'matters theoretical' cf. my "Self-euthanasia, the Dutch experience: in search for the meaning of a good death or eu thanatos", *Bioethics* ISSN 0269-9702 (print); 1467-8519 (online); and "Dementia & Euthanasia: Doubts regarding advanced dementia and advance directive", *Journal of Medical Law and Ethics* Vol. 8, 2020, no. 1, 33-47.

himself. He had always been single and accustomed to making and carrying out his decisions himself.

After studying biology (General biology; Physiology; Endocrinology; Molecular biology; Marine biology), a career followed that took him all over the world: the Netherlands, the Overseas Territories, Suriname, France, Italy, America, Japan, Thailand, India, and so on. A host of honorable invitations and appointments to highly regarded international institutions and an interesting list of publications completed the impression that our conversation could well be an interesting one. In addition, it turned out we shared a way of speaking and writing that may cause problems in ordinary life, i.e., a wide use of irony. It was one of the first things I noticed and had to quickly get used to as well, as it is not a usual thing.

It was also with that sense of irony that Anton looked at our meeting and the few conversations we had, gazing out into a very distant horizon.

He had spent his life alone. Most of his friends had fallen away by now, though there were still two he telephoned regularly, at the hours that were convenient in their parts of the world (America and Africa). He had by now let them know that this regular telephone contact would come to an end fairly soon.

Our duty to ourselves
Anton's decision had been made. Our conversations were certainly not intended as a kind of test or check of his decision. He did, however, want to take advantage of my expertise in order to ensure that things were executed with as much care as possible, before the end of the year. That care included among other things: assuring the use of the right means; assuring a proper execution; proper attention to the person who would find him deceased; and to clearly visible further information because he had made his body available to science. In our three conversations, we talked about all these things, and obviously also about his wish to die, but this in complete freedom. My information was available for him.

At our penultimate meeting, he presented me with a fossil of an Orthoceras, some 200,000,000 years old. On that occasion we were able to establish once again how relative age was and how relative the importance of humankind in the big picture, *sub specie aeternitatis*. And why then should a human being not be allowed to end his life at a self-chosen moment? Maybe because the importance of such life is so great? Here I recalled David Hume in his "Of Suicide" saying… "But the life of man is of no greater importance to the universe than that of an oyster." Since Anton was also familiar with my interview in *Uitweg* (Chabot & Braam[2]), he, for his part, remembered the motto above it taken from the same essay by Hume, and quoted it: "That Suicide may often be consistent with interest and with our duty to *ourselves*, no one can question, who allows, that age, sickness, or misfortune may render life a burthen, and make it worse even than annihilation."

Peaceful
In Anton's eyes, Hume thus gave an apt description of his situation in his 86th year of his life. And he was absolutely at peace with letting go. His last request to "humanity in my person" (after Immanuel Kant; and Anton did not speak without irony), was: would I be prepared to be present at his ending of his life. Not that his farewell would not take place without my being present. There was no doubt. But to have another human being beside him at that moment, "seemed rather pleasant to him".

With or without irony, it remains a serious request. Since my acquittal before the Amsterdam Court (2007[3]), this was the second time I had responded positively to it. The date Anton had set was purposely so well ahead of Christmas that by the time of Christmas everyone could and would have gotten over his voluntary departure. He was happy to take that into account, although he was equally happy to have left before that date.

His life-ending medication was by now in his possession and the pills had also already been crushed, resulting in a quantity of powder in the order of an old-fashioned cylinder for a roll of film. In this cylinder he kept it for the last few days of his life.

Greetings to you all
On the day of his self-euthanasia, I visited Anton in the afternoon as arranged. He was now in pyjamas. We sat for a while in front of the large window, looking out over river and landscape. Heraclitus came by briefly – you can never step in the same river twice – and Epicurus – as long as you are there, death is not there, and when death is there, you are no longer there; so why worry. Then it was time, Anton said.

In his bedroom all the necessities were ready and waiting. Next to the bed a letter with the relevant information for the family doctor and coroner. Information for the notary was laid ready in clear view in the living room,

---

2   Chabot, Boudewijn, i.s.m. Braam, Stella, *Uitweg. Een waardig levenseinde in eigen hand*, Amsterdam: Nijgh & Van Ditmar, 2010, p. 169-175.
3   ECLI:NL:RBAMS:2007:AZ6713.

including an envelope with his last financial obligation to me, plastered with some pictures of finches.

Sitting on his bed – among the greatest of his many physical annoyances was a broken back for which he wore a corset – he took his lethal medication strewn over applesauce. The previous 24 hours he had neatly taken his anti-emetics. When asked how it tasted, he replied that it wasn't too bad. Hardly bitter at all. He drank some more water. Stayed upright for another two or three minutes, but already felt sleep slowly creeping in and laid himself down. We talked for another five minutes or so, but then sleep definitely overtook him.

As agreed, I sat beside him for another forty minutes. I had myself the impression that he had already died by the time I left, but I am not a doctor who can determine this with certainty. I said my final goodbyes to Anton and left the building. As planned, Anton was found deceased the next morning. On his bedroom door, he had affixed a warning, which read in capitals, "Sleeping peacefully: Dr. Anton (...). He has donated his body to the Department of Anatomy, of his Alma Mater, the State University of (...). Greetings to you all, (...)."

And so it was decided, the case of Mr. and Mrs. Meester

Every once in a while a joint self-euthanasia of an elderly couple reaches the press, though it is and remains an exceptional event. With Mr. and Mrs. Meester, both in their eighties, I had an intensive consultation at which their children were also present. All possibilities of gaining control over the end of life were considered. The consultation was not an unnecessary one, and the situation they were in – she was already demented, he in fact still reasonably healthy – was not an easy one. The specter of advanced dementia was looming large in the background, or perhaps it would be better to say: already in the foreground.

What to do? Wait for her to die first – possibly precipitated by a process of stopping eating and drinking – after which he would follow her by his own hand? Or after all, go jointly together? The preference for the latter option in the end prevailed. The necessary – reliable – lethal medication was obtained without difficulty, in this case from Mexico.

We had some further telephone contacts, amongst other things about those lethal drugs. On that subject, I could easily reassure them. The family doctor, who was aware of the couple's intention, also approached me with some questions, out of a sense of responsibility. Him I could reassure as well.

Given the developing dementia, waiting for a longer stretch of time was not an option anymore. Now it was still possible to do it, that is, now she too could still do it herself. And so it was decided, in order not to be too late and in order also to be able to go together.

'And so it was decided ...' This again sounds as if it was simple and easy to decide, but of course it was not, especially not, given the couple's circumstances. You might say that a double dilemma had to be faced here. To begin with, there was the dilemma of Mrs. Meester's developing dementia. This created a pressure: too late in such a case really means too late[4]. And so you have to be early, early enough to be able to still play your executive role. And that means sacrificing time of life. In this case, that was in the first place true for her.

But in addition, there was the desire not to let go of each other. To stay together, until and including death. Given the obvious differences in individual circumstances, this desire also meant sacrificing time of life. More time of life. And this particular sacrifice now clearly had to be made by Mr. Meester.

Taking this kind of complicated decisions is not everyone's cup of tea. Mr. and Mrs. Meester managed to do so. They ended their lives together, and were found lying hand in hand in bed. In a later conversation, one of the children confirmed the peaceful and calm process of the double self-euthanasia. After the arrival of the family doctor and coroner, a prosecutor arrived with about ten more police officers in his wake, events for which I had prepared the next of kin. These officials all cleared the field again after a few hours. After that, the next of kin could do what needed to be done.

Had I gone completely mad?!, the case of Esther Prince

Mrs. Esther Prince was by now well past eighty. In her working life, she had been a psychiatrist. Meanwhile she had – quite literally, as it would later turn out – developed a very fragile physical condition. Mentally, there was little the matter with her. She was perhaps somewhat forgetful, but that hardly meant anything.

She inhabited a beautiful old mansion in Amsterdam, with a spacious basement, which in days gone by housed the servants. Beautiful marble

---

4   A clear example of what this may lead to is given by the only case of physician-euthanasia that went to court in the Netherlands. The physician paid the price for the patient's inability to carry the weight of her own choice. (ECLI:NL:RBDHA:2019:9506; ECLI:NL:HR:2020:712.)

stairs – they would come to play a role yet – led to the upper floors. Below, the first floor, despite the well-maintained woodwork, gave the impression of still being in its old original state. Interesting art hung everywhere. Up two flights of stairs was Esther's bedroom, to which a simple kitchenette had been added for convenience. It was a house she did not wish ever to leave for any nursing home in the world. She had lived a rich life there, together with her long-deceased husband, with whom she had made many beautiful, and sometimes distant, journeys. There were no children.

Fragile but reassured
When Esther contacted me, it was in a fairly down-to-earth manner. She sensed that the moment of physical decline that might create a permanent obstacle was approaching. She wanted to be ahead of that moment at all costs. For this reason we made an appointment for a first meeting. We spoke downstairs. She told me about her life, her former work, her late husband, her travels, her vision of life. She could tell interesting stories.

But of course that's not what I came for. We talked at length about how she could take control and be in charge of her end of life, with a self-composed lethal 'pill'. It was all very quickly clear to her. Getting the appropriate lethal medication was in those days not going to be a problem for her either. And that was indeed true; they were delivered punctually at her very door.

Our conversation took place just after summer vacation, and from then on she felt reassured. The question, of course, was: when would she decide to make her move? She certainly wasn't in a hurry, but worries about being overtaken by the facts she did have. Her physical condition, as mentioned, was very fragile.

During our conversation, she had also asked me if I would be prepared to be with her when she took her step out of life. Since that was not an actual issue at that very moment of time, the question remained unanswered. I did not say no; we would return to the matter later. Time passed and the year slowly drew to a close. In December, she contacted me again: was I still there? Yes, I was still there. And was I still available? Yes, and after the holidays we would make a new appointment. She was clearly feeling weaker, and the time for her to act was approaching. At least that was what I thought I heard in her message.

Faster
And then it all moved even faster. She soon after called me again asking if I could and would come the day before Christmas. And no, not for just

another conversation, but for a final conversation that would culminate in her stepping out of life. Her condition was clearly deteriorating. She was forced to stay in bed a lot and drew her conclusions.

I had to think about this request for a moment. I also had to consult – it was Christmas! – with the home front, but after that the answer was clear: "OK, I'm coming. But do take it all very easy!"

As she would probably be in bed and would not easily be able to quickly come all the way downstairs on my ringing the doorbell, she wanted to solve this by leaving a side-door that provided access to the basement unlocked. This way I could enter by myself upon arrival. The grocer also put his groceries there.

This being arranged, I travelled to Amsterdam. The door was indeed unlocked and I climbed the few steps from the basement to the first floor, toward the stairs that led upstairs. And there, four or five steps from the bottom, I found Esther, lying on the marble stairs. She had come down the two stairs from the bedroom to unlock the basement door. On the way back up, she had slipped and fallen on the marble stairs. As far as I could see, she had been lying there for some time, in her nightgown, on a cold marble staircase, presumably with a broken hip.

Mad?

The first thing that occurred to me was: we're going to call for help. What's the number of the doctor's office? But her reaction was quite different: "Ho, ho! Had I gone completely mad?!" That was exactly what wasn't supposed to happen! Surely that was not what she had asked me to come for, was it? And indeed, even though I insisted a bit at first, I had to acknowledge: she had a point.

But what to do next? In any case, Esther had to climb the two stairs to her bedroom, where her lethal medication – fortunately, as it turned out later, fully prepared – was waiting for her on her bedside table. But how? Her walking stick was no longer of any use to her. She was frail and small. We agreed on how we were going to do it. I would stand in front of her and sink through my knees. Then she would put her arms around my neck, and I would slowly get up. Doing so, we would then find out if she could handle it, and how her hip would behave.

And so it was done. Esther hung around my neck, and I lifted her, taking her step by step up the two flights of stairs. Her weight was no problem. In her bedroom I put her on the bed, after which she carefully worked her way under the covers and finally got a little warm again.

To die peacefully

We took time for her to recover somewhat. Needless to say, the situation had caught me very off guard. Only now did I notice how well-groomed she looked. Neatly coiffed, painted nails, and makeup. All in order to be able to die in style.

She was in pain and asked a question I won't soon forget: "Would it hurt if she took two paracetamol?" I said, concerned about her pain, "As far as I'm concerned, you take six of them." But no, certainly not, she wouldn't, out of the question. Her stomach had to stand up to her lethal medication. In the end, the pain was secondary. Another interest was paramount: being able to die peacefully.

And that's what happened. First we took some time to talk a bit and catch up. After she had recovered and was warm and comfortable again, she took her bowl of yogurt from her bedside table, stirred in the ready-made and already crushed medication, and emptied the bowl.

For another five minutes or so we were able to talk to each other clearly, after which talking became increasingly difficult for her, until sleep took over. As agreed, I stayed with her for about another forty-five minutes 'keeping watch'. Then I greeted Esther one last time and descended the marble steps again. Out into the Christmas atmosphere.

A few days later, I received a phone call from the person who was scheduled to find Esther the morning following her self-euthanasia. He informed me that he had found her lying peacefully deceased in her bed.

About the author

Ton Vink (tonvink@ninewells.nl) worked as a counselor for end-of-life issues for over twenty years. In 2007 he was acquitted before the Amsterdam Court of violating art. 294 of the Criminal Code, Assistance with suicide (ECLI:NL:RBAMS:2007:AZ6713).

For Product Safety Concerns and Information please contact our EU
representative GPSR@taylorandfrancis.com
Taylor & Francis Verlag GmbH, Kaufingerstraße 24, 80331 München, Germany

www.ingramcontent.com/pod-product-compliance
Lightning Source LLC
Chambersburg PA
CBHW051103230426
43667CB00013B/2425